cry sorrow, cry joy!

SELECTIONS FROM CONTEMPORARY AFRICAN WRITERS

edited by Jane Ann Moore

FRIENDSHIP PRESS • NEW YORK

When the man
who knows no disasters
hears weeping—
he thinks it is song

—*A Yoruba Proverb*

Library of Congress Catalogue Card Number: 74–146632

Copyright © 1971 by Friendship Press, Inc.
Printed in the United States of America

contents

INTRODUCTION
Home and Exile, Lewis Nkosi   12

FAMILY
No Longer at Ease, Chinua Achebe   20
The Interpreters, Wole Soyinka   29
Beautiful Feathers,
    Cyprian Ekwensi   34
The Opportunity, Arthur Maimane   38

EDUCATION
Tell Freedom, Peter Abrahams   56
Weep Not, Child, James Ngugi   64
America, Their America, J. P. Clark   76
I Will Try, Legson Kayira   80

POLITICS
People of the City,
    Cyprian Ekwensi   90
No Easy Task, Aubrey Kachingwe   93
Beautiful Feathers,
    Cyprian Ekwensi   99
The Beautyful Ones Are Not Yet
    Born, Ayi Kwei Armah   103

ECONOMICS
Kinsman and Foreman, T. M. Aluko   119

Weep Not, Child, James Ngugi — 131
Mine Boy, Peter Abrahams — 136
The Gab Boys, Cameron Duodu — 141
The Interpreters, Wole Soyinka — 150

RACE
Houseboy, Ferdinand Oyono — 162
"Telephone Conversation,"
    Wole Soyinka — 164
Papa, the Snake and I,
    Luis Bernardo Honwana — 165
The Park, James Matthews — 170
The Living and the Dead,
    Ezekiel Mphahlele — 185

RELIGION
The African Child, Camara Laye — 195
The Catechist,
    Joseph W. Abruquah — 197
Down Second Avenue,
    Ezekiel Mphahlele — 209
24 Poems,
    Jean-Joseph Rabearivelo — 217
A Grain of Wheat, James Ngugi — 218

**BIOGRAPHICAL INFORMATION
ON AFRICAN WRITERS** — 220

introduction

Today non-Africans have an unparalled opportunity to see Africa through African eyes. Fifteen years ago there were few writings by African artists in Western languages. Since then we have had placed before us hundreds of literary expressions by black Africans.

This literature fills a yawning void for Africans also—helping them construct new self-images, positions in society and meanings of life.

Great artists convey the universal condition of man in particular situations. The universal element is readily apparent: whether it is a ten-year-old boy discovering that books hold stories, a teen-ager being chased by the police, a woman finding out her husband wants another wife or an aged pastor trying to talk theology with a young man.

All these human predicaments are complicated by what the white world has done to the black world, by what the rich nations have done to the poor nations, by what the Christian societies have done to societies with other religious beliefs.

In James Ngugi's novel, *A Grain of Wheat,* during the war that white settlers in Kenya called "Mau Mau," a Kikuyu husband was "detained" without trial by whites in a concentration camp for seven years and forbidden any communication with his wife. When they finally have the opportunity to speak to each other, the wife says, "Too much has happened to be passed over in a sentence." Immediate reunion is not possible yet. Reconciliation can take place only when a shared understanding of what has passed is accepted; when there is the will to forge a new, equal relationship; when a plan for the future is in sight.

This impasse between husband and wife is symbolic of the relationship between Africa and the West. There is increasing separation between black and white. Immediate reconciliation is not possible. One has injured the other. One has misruled the other. One has libeled the other. Now is the time to share in the cry of what has happened to Africa.

These stories contain many kinds of cries. The Dutch philosopher, Willem Zuurdeeg, urges us to pay special attention to a cry. "A man may become genuinely human when he cries out in anguish, triumph, in furious rebellion and in joyful reverence." Such crying, he says, is an act almost unavailable to Western man because, for us, a cry is not a respectable mode of behavior. He asks, "Who can live by a cry? Who can stand it to hear such disturbing noise?" The creative artist can live by crying out in his writing. The creative reader can stand it to listen. As Africans cry aloud in their literature, one can hear them give new personal, social and cultural definition to themselves and to those with ears to listen.

PERSONAL DEFINITION

In a racist society the black child sees others looking at him; he sees them making judgments: he believes them. The short story by James Matthews, "The Park," tells how a little African boy's looking-glass image of himself is formed. In the eyes of those who count, he is worthless. Colonialism, discrimination, apartheid—all these forces in Africa have inflicted grave wounds upon the black self. Can literature undo in any way these detrimental images of the self?

Lewis Nkosi, a South African writer who grew up in that little boy's world, believes that literature *does* have the power to mold life. But until the last dozen years there were no literary heroes with whom young Africans could identify. Novels by white men, by Graham Greene and Joyce Cary, skilled though they were in portraying white colonial society, used Africa only as an exotic backdrop and stuck in a few caricatures of black Africans. These novels provided only negative stereotypes for black Africans—but no sense of identity.

For decades our African heroes have been white. One, Albert Schweitzer, seems to have been more concerned about the universal human struggle of the soul than about the particularity of the African soul. Another, Alan Paton, seems in his first novel, *Cry, the Beloved Country,* to be more concerned to reach the conscience of "white liberals" with the injustice of South Africa than to reach the psyche of African youths. Useful as their contributions to Africans have been, these white heroes did not provide the new generation of Africans with positive models of identity. They did bring the continent to our attention; but today there are black writers who can take us into its heartland!

Recalling his own youth, Lewis Nkosi says that

". . . when we entered the decade of the fifties we had no literary heroes, like generations in other parts of the world. We had to improvise because there were no models who could serve as moral examples for us. . . [as] a generation we longed desperately for literary heroes we could respect and with whom we could identify. In the moral chaos through which we were living we longed to find a work of literature, a drama or film, home-grown and about us, which would contain a sig-nificant amount of our experience and in which we could find our own attitudes and feelings." [1]

The stories herein contain many models for youth.

SOCIAL DEFINITION

Most of these stories deal with the African's search for a place in the new African society. "What shall I be when I grow up?" asks the Afri-can child. "Rich man, poor man, beggarman, thief? Doctor, lawyer, merchant, chief?" "What is my place in my nation?" asks the young adult.

"Shall I live a traditional woman's life in the village or be a liberated woman of the city? Shall I accept the lowly job of catechist or struggle to become a minister? Shall I keep the high standards of engineering I learned at the European univer-sity or give in to the corrupt recommendations of

[1] From *Home and Exile*, Copyright © Lewis Nkosi, 1965. Reprinted by permission of Longman Group, Ltd. and Deborah Rogers, Ltd., London.

the expatriate expert who lies for profit? Shall I be an elitist African puppet selling my people to the neocolonialists or sink into emotional illness because I am unable to help my own people? Shall I enter a privileged profession or go back to the villages to aid the rural poor?" These writings can thus be seen as self-conscious descriptions of the role conflicts in their societies.

Many African writers are young men wrestling with these very questions, not only in their writings but in their lives. What is the place of the African writer himself? Is he a neutral observor? Is he an entertainer for white book buyers? Is he a mental patient using writing as therapy against his disillusionment with white and black hypocrisy? Is he a gentle defender, insisting politely that Africans *did* have a past of their own—a civilization, a religion, a history? Is he a moralist, denouncing his own countrymen's politicians because they are not doing what they had agreed they should on behalf of the people? Is he a cartographer-of-the-future, exclaiming: "Let's not waste too much time explaining what we were and pleading with some people and telling them we are also human. Let us forget that; let us map out what we are going to be tomorrow. . . . Our most meaningful job today should be to determine what kind of society we want, how we are going to get there, what values we can take from the past, if we can, as we move along." [2] Is he a violent revolutionary seeing hope only in the destruction of present racist governments still ruling in Africa? In this anthology there are writers who speak from most of these stances.

[2] Lindfars, Bernth, "Achebe on Commitment and African Writers," *Africa Report*, March 1970, p. 18. Reprinted by permission.

CULTURAL DEFINITION

"Africa has suffered more than any other continent," states novelist Ayi Kwei Armah. From 1442 to 1880, 69,000,000 Africans were captured by European slavers, put on ships, chained, closed in under the deck, sporadically fed and left to defecate and urinate on themselves. One-third of them survived the trip. The Western world knows very little about African suffering. Jews past and present have suffered greatly too; but in contrast their suffering is well-known through Europe and North America. Why do we know the suffering of the Jewish people, but not the suffering of Africa?

One reason is that the Jews wrote down their own history, a history that stressed political defeat and dispersion as much as it stressed victory and empire, in the Old Testament where it was available to everyone in the West to read. Today Africans are writing down their history, containing such epics as the building of the Mali, Ghana and Songhay empires. Information comes from oral tradition, archeology and archives of Islamic and other scholars. African historians are retelling their war stories, such as the placing in battle of 200,000 warriors of Ghana in 1066 A.D., the same year in which the Normans could muster only 15,000 soldiers to invade England. And also they are chronicling their defeats at the hands of all the colonial powers. It was the genius of the Jewish people that they took their experiences of suffering and made them the cohesive core that strengthened their common bonds for centuries.

In this collection of African stories there are many interpretations of African suffering: knowledge of evil, reality of injustice, loneliness away from parents, destroyed love, self-awareness, bitterness, ethnocentrism, tyranny, corruption, brokenness. In Soyinka's *The Interpreters* the response of college friends to the suicide of a brilliant colleague is one of despair: "Sekoni's death had left them all wet, bedraggled, the paint running down their acceptance of life where they thought the image was set. . . ." But there is also hope. The extent of Africans' suffering and the uniqueness of their situation gives a unique shape to their hopes.

In Africa many religious, intellectual and political movements have attracted followers with the promise of hope. Spiritualist groups have promised release from suffering. Renascent indigenous religions have purified themselves of what they consider Western taint. Islam has promised acceptance of the black race as equal. Secularism has rejected the white man's Trinity. Independent Christian churches have sought release from a white hierarchy. "Negritude" has asserted that black is most beautiful and Africa the source of goodness. "African personality" has claimed that the whole man is superior to the overly intellectualized people of the West. Right now the word on many lips is Pan-Africanism. Once, this term referred to the political unification of the dozens of African states. Today it incorporates a creed including concern for deprived Africans everywhere, unity of all black peoples, responsibility of one African for another and the need to organize black people beyond the limitations of tribalism.

Out of this suffering and in this hope, Africans are redefining the meaning of their continent.

Before we read these selections, we must ask:

Have we, the West, the right to intrude into the innermost reaches of the African heart? Have African writers any responsibility to tell us their experiences? Some of them are saying today: "Do not write in English any more. Do not publish in the West. Rule out expensive bindings. Cease appealing to Western titillations. Write only for Africa." They suspect what we will do with our knowledge. They are asking: "Will we fashion our foreign policy ever more cleverly? Will we plan our trade more exploitatively? Will we convert more expeditiously? Will we ensnare the African elite more totally?" Will we exploit them further as they fear, or will we begin to build bridges of reconciliation?"

Home and Exile
Lewis Nkosi

My generation came to maturity just before or soon after the Second World War, at about the same time that Dr. Malan was taking over the country on a mandate to apply more rigidly apartheid than the Smuts Government before him had seemed prepared to do. It could not therefore without some superhuman effort understand the naive credulity of its elders. Though we doubted we could have done any better in the circumstances, we were nonetheless bitter that our great

From *Home and Exile*, Copyright © Lewis Nkosi, 1965. Reprinted by permission of Longman Group, Ltd. and Deborah Rogers, Ltd., London.

grandfathers had lost a country to the whites. It was therefore with genuine pain that we were prepared to forgive them their ignoble defeat.

What we were not, by any means, prepared to forgive was the indecent readiness with which our immediate elders were prepared to believe that after this history of war and pillage white people meant well by us, and that given time they would soon accord us equal say in the running of the country's affairs. Not only had our elders apparently believed this patent hoax but during the Second World War they had allowed themselves to be pressed into service under the impression that they were helping win freedom and democracy for *us!* This seemed to us incredible stupidity. . . .

The evidence of their writing was not the least encouraging. When we turned to their literature our sense of outrage was sharpened. . . .

We, the young, were blamed, of course, not only for having defected from the time-tested morality of the tribe but were also sharply reprimanded for refusing *at least* to substitute a Christian morality in its place. Often enough—I think with some truth—we were accused of being irresponsible, cynical, pleasure-loving, world-weary and old before our time had arrived to be truly old. Most vernacular novels, as well as those written in English, novels upon which we were nourished in our boyhood, worked and reworked the theme of *Jim Comes To Jo-burg* [1] in which it was implied that Jim's loss of place in the tightly woven tribal structure and the corresponding attenu-

---

[1] A film of the same title was produced in Johannesburg in the early fifties, portraying a tribal innocent who succumbs to the temptations of city life.

ation of the elders' authority over him was the main cause rather than the result of the nation's tragedy. Jim's disaffiliation from the tribe in favour of the self-seeking individualistic ethos of urban life, we were made to understand, was tantamount to Jim's loss of manhood. As a matter of fact, this was the subservient theme in Alan Paton's *Cry, the Beloved Country*.

If we rejected Stephen Kumalo, Paton's hero, it was partly because we, the young, suspected that the priest was a cunning expression of white liberal sentiment. Paton's generosity of spirit, his courageous plea for racial justice, and all those qualities which have earned him the undying respect of many Africans, were not of course in question. What was in question was Paton's method, his fictional control of African character which produced an ultimate absurdity like Stephen Kumalo: an embodiment of all the pieties, trepidations and humilities we the young had begun to despise with such a consuming passion.

We thought we discerned in Stephen Kumalo's naivete and simple-minded goodwill, white South Africa's subconscious desire to survive the blind tragedy which was bound to engulf the country sooner or later; for if the African (or anybody else for that matter) was as fundamentally good and forgiving as Stephen Kumalo was conceived by Paton to be, then the white South Africans might yet escape the immense penalty which they would be required to pay.

You will remember that Kumalo, the priest who goes to Johannesburg in search of his son, is afforded ample opportunity to witness the moral decay of the society for which the major responsibility must surely lie with the racist exploiters. But strangely enough, if somewhat unconvincingly, this is the kind of Gethsemane from which Kumalo emerges without moral profit to return once more to Indotsheni, his innocence still intact, as convinced as ever that there is nothing fundamentally wrong with the society which cannot be set right by love and prayer. Caught as he is in the Christian liberal's dilemma of how to persuade an unwilling people to change for the good without a recourse to revolution or a certain amount of force, Paton's novel can only end with a distorted, sentimental, if meliorative vision, in which reconciliation consists of liberals supplying milk and helping build a dam in a Bantustan. However, this optimism, then as now, was false, infantile. We had to wait for the publication of Paton's *Tales from a Troubled Land,* a record, I would say, of Paton's actual experience and therefore an unsentimentalised encounter with the dark and iron reality of the life of the urban African, to witness, finally, Paton's earnest confrontation of the central issue of Evil and the meagreness of the liberal vision before so challenging a reality. . . .

. . . Stephen Kumalo seems to me quite incredible and I would say he is quite easy to repudiate, for as a character he is no more than a figment of a white liberal's imagination. Where so many white South African writers fall flat on their faces in their effort to portray the so-called simple African is in their inability to see and underline the fantastic ambiguity, the deliberate self-deception, the ever-present irony beneath the mock humility and moderation of speech. It is this irony of the subtle persecution of a white man by a so-called simple African which is the supreme achievement of Dan Jacobson's *The Trap.*

We, the young, also despised Stephen Kumalo,
of course, for his failure to come to terms with the
city; we despised him even more heartily when he
'copped out,' retreating finally to Indotsheni; and
we despised him right up to the moment he
climbed the mountain to offer that extraordinary
prayer to God, which was really the prayer of a
man in a deep panic, a man, nonetheless, who is
not permitted even the dignity of a minimum
awareness and comprehension of his situation.

I write so much at length about the hero of
Alan Paton's novel not in any effort to give a full
critique of the novel as a work of art, but in order
to show that when we entered the decade of the
fifties we had no literary heroes, like generations
in other parts of the world. We had to improvise
because there were no models who could serve as
moral examples for us in our private and public
preoccupations. On the other hand by the time we
were through living in the fifties we had given
white writers a milieu and characters who were
recognisably modelled upon our lives. Several associates working for DRUM magazine individually
and collectively made up the characters and provided the social milieu of stories like Paton's
Drink in the Passage, or Nadine Gordimer's *A
World of Strangers* and *Occasion for Loving.*
Paton's story is, in fact, a report of what actually
happened in real life to one of us.

I know that for those who do not believe in the
power of literature to mould life and manners the
need for literary heroes must seem not only silly
but self-indulgent; nevertheless it seems to me that
as a generation we longed desperately for literary
heroes we could respect and with whom we could
identify. In the moral chaos through which we

were living we longed to find a work of literature, a drama or film, home-grown and about us, which would contain a significant amount of our experience and in which we could find our own attitudes and feelings. For a generation reaching maturity, it was an intolerable strain not to have our own Holden Caulfield against whom to measure our own feelings and test our vision of reality. I suppose, in a sense, the war between us and Stephen Kumalo was therefore a war between two generations—the older generation which looked forward to fruitful changes under the Smuts Government and the young who saw themselves beginning their adult life under a more brutal apartheid regime.

family

It used to be said there were two kinds of family life in Africa: traditional and Western. But African novelists describe many more styles of life.

In Achebe's No Longer at Ease, a rural Christian home is described. The father is a catechist of the Anglican Church. His wife is a convert though her thought patterns remain traditional. The father is dedicated to Western education but is caught in indigenous prejudices against osus, religious functionaries who have been outcasts in Ibo society for many generations. The parents are devoted to each other in an ideal monogamous way. Their knowledge is limited to rural eastern Nigeria.

In the same story Obi and Clara want to establish an urban professional home in Lagos, Nigeria. Clara is a graduate nurse. Obi has a position in the Senior Civil Service. Both were educated in England. They visit their home villages out of filial obligation but prefer socializing with colleagues. Their religion is secular, universal, cosmopolitan.

In Soyinka's The Interpreters, Dehinwa's

mother may well come from an urban polygamous home (*although other wives are not mentioned*). *In any case, this independent wife has her own successful marketing business and pays her own and the university expenses of her daughter. Extended family loyalties are most important in this type of family. Often the urban polygamous family suffers displacements: wives may not live together in the same compound as they would in the village. A younger "parlor" wife may enjoy the entertaining and traveling in town, with the older wife caring for all the children. By contrast, in the* rural polygamous home *the senior wife would enjoy the seniority privileges.*

In the same story the young Dehinwa and Sagoe want an urban professional home. *They also hope to establish an inter-ethnic marriage in Lagos or Ibadan. He is Hausa. She is Yoruba. He is a journalist. She is a civil servant.*

Wilson and Yaniya in Ekwensi's Beautiful Feathers *are also from different ethnic groups. Wilson is from Northern Nigeria; Yaniya is from Benin in the south. Wilson is a pharmacist, but without an overseas degree. Yaniya has not attended a university, but is mobile in society. They are not yet among the elite of Lagos society, but through Wilson's political organizing, they are widely known. They fit into the lower echelons of the* urban professional *category.*

In Arthur Maimane's play of Ghanaian life in 1956, The Opportunity, *Solomon and Emma belong to the older generation. Apparently Solomon has some formal education, but Emma is barely literate. They rise within one generation's span from the countryside to the city, from unemployment to high position in government. Here is a*

common situation: great disparity in the education
of husband and wife, and tremendous change
within the home of one couple during their own
lifetimes.

An older style of marriage popular among the
coastal, educated and traveled black families was
the urban Victorian Christian home. *Monogamy,*
Victorian manners, virtues and values were highly
prized by the tiny group of professionals who
lived this way. *The British colonial policy had led*
to the growth of the still-small group that lived in
an urban Christian home (1840s to 1880s)—and
it was the British who choked off the growth in
this class through their change in policies (1880s
to World War II). Suddenly British colonialists,
traders and missionary societies changed their pol-
icies and demoted these African professionals and
prevented further promotions, thus causing a re-
duction in the number of Africans who lived in
this Victorian kind of home. However, a remnant
of this amazing group of nineteenth century pro-
fessionals has managed to survive in the cities.

No Longer at Ease
Chinua Achebe

Although he had two weeks, he proposed to
spend only one at home for reasons of money. To
home people, leave meant the return of the village

From *No Longer at Ease,* © Chinua Achebe, 1960. Reprinted by permission of Astor-Honor, Inc., Stamford,
Connecticut and William Heinemann, Ltd., London.

boy who had made good in the town, and everyone expected to share in his good fortune. 'After
all,' they argued, 'it was our prayers and our liba-
tions that did it for him.' They called leave *lifu,*
meaning *to squander.*

Obi had exactly thirty-four pounds, nine and
threepence when he set out. Twenty-five pounds
was his local leave allowance, which was paid to
all senior Civil Servants for no other reason than
that they went on local leave. The rest was the
remains of his January salary. With thirty-four
pounds one might possibly last two weeks at
home, although a man like Obi, with a car and a
'European post,' would normally be expected to
do better. But sixteen pounds ten shillings was to
go into brother John's school fees for the second
term which began in April. Obi knew that unless
he paid the fees now that he had a lump sum in his
pocket he might not be able to do so when the
time came.

* * *

Obi seemed to look over the shoulders of everyone who came out to welcome him home.

'Where is Mother?' his eyes kept asking. He did
not know whether she was still in hospital or at
home, and he was afraid to ask.

'Your mother returned from hospital last week,'
said his father as they entered the house.

'Where is she?'

'In her room,' said Eunice, his youngest sister.

Mother's room was the most distinctive in the
whole house, except perhaps for Father's. The
difficulty in deciding arose from the fact that one
could not compare incomparable things. Mr.
Okonkwo believed utterly and completely in the

things of the white man. And the symbol of the white man's power was the written word, or better still, the printed word. Once before he went to England, Obi heard his father talk with deep feeling about the mystery of the written word to an illiterate kinsman:

'Our women made black patterns on their bodies with the juice of the *uli* tree. It was beautiful, but it soon faded. If it lasted two market weeks it lasted a long time. But sometimes our elders spoke about *uli* that never faded, although no one had ever seen it. We see it today in the writing of the white man. If you go to the native court and look at the books which clerks wrote twenty years ago or more, they are still as they wrote them. They do not say one thing today and another tomorrow, or one thing this year and another next year. Okoye in the book today cannot become Okonkwo tomorrow. In the Bible Pilate said: "What is written is written." It is *uli* that never fades.'

The kinsman had nodded his head in approval and snapped his fingers.

The result of Okonkwo's mystic regard for the written word was that his room was full of old books and papers—from Blackie's *Arithmetic* which he used in 1908 to Obi's Durrell, from obsolete cockroach-eaten translations of the Bible into the Onitsha dialect to yellowed Scripture Union Cards of 1920 and earlier. Okonkwo never destroyed a piece of paper. He had two boxes full of them. The rest were preserved on top of his enormous cupboard, on tables, on boxes and on one corner of the floor.

Mother's room, on the other hand, was full of mundane things. She had her box of clothes on a stool. On the other side of the room were pots of solid palm-oil with which she made black soap.

The palm-oil was separated from the clothes by the whole length of the room, because, as she always said, clothes and oil were not kinsmen, and just as it was the duty of clothes to try and avoid oil it was also the duty of the oil to do everything to avoid clothes.

Apart from these two, Mother's room also had such things as last year's coco yams, kola nuts preserved with banana leaves in empty oil pots, palm-ash preserved in an old cylindrical vessel which, as the older children told Obi, had once contained biscuits. In the second stage of its life it had served as a water vessel until it sprang about five leaks which had to be carefully covered with paper before it got its present job. . . .

* * *

Obi's serious talks with his father began after the family had prayed and all but the two of them had gone to bed. . . .

'Come to my room then,' said his father, leading the way with the ancient hurricane lamp. There was a small table in the middle of the room. Obi remembered when it was bought. Carpenter Moses had built it and offered it to the church at harvest. It was put up for auction after the Harvest Service and sold. He could not now remember how much his father had paid for it, eleven and threepence perhaps. . . .

'. . . You wrote to me some time ago about a girl you had seen. How does the matter stand now?'

'That is one reason why I came. I want us to go and meet her people and start negotiations. I have no money now, but at least we can begin to talk.' Obi had decided that it would be fatal to sound apologetic or hesitant.

'Yes,' said his father. 'That is the best way.' He thought a little and again said yes, it was the best way. Then a new thought seemed to occur to him. 'Do we know who this girl is and where she comes from?' Obi hesitated just enough for his father to ask the question again in a different way. 'What is her name?'

'She is the daughter of Okeke, a native of Mbaino.'

'Which Okeke? I know about three. One is a retired teacher, but it would not be that one.'

'That is the one,' said Obi.

'Josiah Okeke?'

Obi said, yes, that was his name.

His father laughed. It was the kind of laughter one sometimes heard from a masked ancestral spirit. He would salute you by name and ask you if you knew who he was. You would reply with one hand humbly touching the ground that you did not, that he was beyond human knowledge. Then he might laugh as if through a throat of metal. And the meaning of that laughter was clear: 'I did not really think you would know, you miserable human worm!'

Obi's father's laughter vanished as it had come —without warning, leaving no footprints.

'You cannot marry the girl,' he said quite simply.

'Eh?'

'I said you cannot marry the girl.'

'But why, Father?'

'Why? I shall tell you why. But first tell me this. Did you find out or try to find out anything about this girl?'

'Yes.'

'What did you find out?'

'That they are *osu*.'

'You mean to tell me that you knew, and you ask me why?'

'I don't think it matters. We are Christians.' This had some effect, nothing startling though. Only a little pause and a slightly softer tone.

'We are Christians,' he said. 'But that is no reason to marry an *osu*.'

'The Bible says that in Christ there are no bond or free.'

'My son,' said Okonkwo, 'I understand what you say. But this thing is deeper than you think.'

'What is *this thing*? Our fathers in their darkness and ignorance called an innocent man *osu*, a thing given to idols, and thereafter he became an outcast, and his children, and his children's children for ever. But have we not seen the light of the Gospel?' Obi used the very words that his father might have used in talking to his heathen kinsmen.

There was a long silence. The lamp was now burning too brightly. Obi's father turned down the wick a little and then resumed his silence. After what seemed ages he said: 'I know Josiah Okeke very well.' He was looking steadily in front of him. His voice sounded tired. 'I know him and I know his wife. He is a good man and a great Christian. But he is *osu*. Naaman, captain of the host of Syria, was a great man and honourable, he was also a mighty man of valour, but he was a leper.' He paused so that this great and felicitous analogy might sink in with all its heavy and dreadful weight.

'*Osu* is like leprosy in the minds of our people. I beg of you, my son, not to bring the mark of shame and of leprosy into your family. If you do, your children and your children's children unto the third and fourth generations will curse your memory. It is not for myself I speak; my days are few. You will bring sorrow on your head and on the heads of your children. Who will marry your daughters? Whose daughters will your sons marry? Think of that, my son. We are Christians, but we cannot marry our own daughters.'

'But all that is going to change. In ten years things will be quite different to what they are now.'

The old man shook his head sadly but said no more. Obi repeated his points again. What made an *osu* different from other men and women? Nothing but the ignorance of their forefathers. Why should they, who had seen the light of the Gospel, remain in that ignorance?

He slept very little that night. His father had not appeared as difficult as he had expected. He had not been won over yet, but he had clearly weakened. Obi felt strangely happy and excited. He had not been through anything quite like this before. He was used to speaking to his mother like an equal, even from his childhood, but his father had always been different. He was not exactly remote from his family, but there was something about him that made one think of the patriarchs, those giants hewn from granite. Obi's strange happiness sprang not only from the little ground he had won in the argument, but from the direct human contact he had made with his father for the first time in his twenty-six years.

* * *

As soon as he woke up in the morning he went to see his mother. It was six o'clock by his watch, but still very dark. He groped his way to her room. She was awake, for she asked who it was as soon as he entered the room. He went and sat on her bed and felt her temperature with his palm. She had not slept much on account of the pain in her stomach. She said she had now lost faith in the European medicine and would like to try a native doctor.

At that moment Obi's father rang his little bell to summon the family to morning prayers. He was surprised when he came in with the lamp and saw Obi already there. Eunice came in wrapped up in her loin-cloth. She was the last of the children and the only one at home. That was what the world had come to. Children left their old parents at home and scattered in all directions in search of money. It was hard on an old woman with eight children. It was like having a river and yet washing one's hands with spittle. . . .

Afterwards, when they were alone again, she listened silently and patiently to the end. Then she raised herself up and said: 'I dreamt a bad dream, a very bad dream one night. I was lying on a bed spread with white cloth and I felt something creepy against my skin. I looked down on the bed and found that a swarm of white termites had eaten it up, and the mat and the white cloth. Yes, termites had eaten up the bed right under me.'

A strange feeling like cold dew descended on Obi's head.

'I did not tell anybody about that dream in the morning. I carried it in my heart wondering what it was. I took down my Bible and read the portion for the day. It gave me some strength, but my heart was still not at rest. In the afternoon your father came in with a letter from Joseph to tell us that you were going to marry an *osu*. I saw the meaning of my death in the dream. Then I told your father about it.' She stopped and took a deep breath. 'I have nothing to tell you in this matter except one thing. If you want to marry this girl,

you must wait until I am no more. If God hears
my prayers, you will not wait long.' She stopped
again. Obi was terrified by the change that had
come over her. She looked strange as if she had
suddenly gone off her head.

'Mother!' he called, as if she was going away.
She held up her hand for silence.

'But if you do the thing while I am alive, you
will have my blood on your head, because I shall
kill myself.' She sank down completely exhausted.

* * *

'I shall return to Lagos the day after tomorrow,'
Obi said finally.

'Did you not say you had a week to spend with
us?'

'Yes, but I think it will be better if I return
earlier.'

After this there was another long silence. Then
his father spoke, but not about the thing that was
on their minds. He began slowly and quietly, so
quietly that his words were barely audible. It
seemed as if he was not really speaking to Obi.
His face was turned sideways so that Obi saw it in
vague profile.

'I was no more than a boy when I left my father's house and went with the missionaries. He
placed a curse on me. I was not there but my
brothers told me it was true. When a man curses
his own child it is a terrible thing. And I was his
first son.'

Obi had never heard about the curse. In broad
daylight and in happier circumstances he would
not have attached any importance to it. But that
night he felt strangely moved with pity for his
father.

'When they brought me word that he had

hanged himself I told them that those who live by
the sword must perish by the sword. Mr Bradde-
ley, the white man who was our teacher, said it
was not the right thing to say and told me to go
home for the burial. I refused to go. Mr. Bradde-
ley thought I spoke about the white man's messenger whom my father killed. He did not know I
spoke about Ikemefuna with whom I grew up in
my mother's hut until the day came when my father killed him with his own hands.' He paused to
collect his thoughts, turned in his chair and faced
the bed on which Obi lay. 'I tell you all this so
that you may know what it was in those days to
become a Christian. I left my father's house, and
he placed a curse on me. I went through fire to become a Christian. Because I suffered I understand
Christianity—more than you will ever do.' He
stopped rather abruptly. Obi thought it was a
pause, but he had finished. . . .

The Interpreters
Wole Soyinka

Dehinwa stood with the key in her hand,
thoughtful. 'A woman? You are sure it was a
woman? . . . It would be my mother. She and
some relations, I am certain. And God, I am so
tired.'

As she opened the door a figure rose from the
gloom, a black shawl slipped down and an enor-

From *The Interpreters*, © 1965 by Wole Soyinka. Reprinted by permission of Andre Deutsch, Ltd., London.

mous head-tie bristled. Sagoe fell backwards, hitting his head against the balustrade. All went dark but for a few moments he heard voices from Gehenna . . .

'So Dehinwa, this is what you people do in Lagos . . . is this a decent time for a young girl to be out?'

'Ah Mamma . . . and auntie too . . . I am so sorry. Have you been waiting long?' . . .

. . . Once her mother had travelled to see her, arriving late in the night. Then Dehinwa's mind still ran to reasons. To reasonable reasons, disasters, emergencies. That time her mind flew to a grandfather who had been in hospital for some time. It was nothing of the sort. Not that time, not this, not any other time.

'Why mother, what is the matter?'

The mother settled herself and asked if she had tea in the house. . . . She never came alone, perhaps she sensed a change, some time of decisions when an aunt's moral support would count for much. Inevitably it was an indigent aunt or cousin who could be hustled down to Lagos at the moment's notice, one who sat and sighed and chorused 'For your own good; listen my child, what your mother says is for your own good. We had no one to tell us these things, so count yourself lucky.'

The tea was made and the aunt asked for bread with sardines. 'I had no time to eat, you see. Would I stop to eat where my own children were concerned? Not likely. And what touches your mother touches me. I regard you as my own children. Oh, perhaps some stew then, if you have no sardines . . .'

The aunt, sucking steaming tea as through a

straw began, 'Your mother's *aladura* had a vision concerning you.' Tension in the mother more than the heat raised huge drops of sweat on her face. The aunt scooped hot peppers with the bread, began to sweat in sympathy. 'Your mother was very worried. She chartered a taxi and called on me to accompany her. As you see, we are here. This is what brought us.'

'What was this vision?' Dehinwa wanted to know.

'He saw you brought to bed. You gave me a grandson.'

Dehinwa could not help smiling. 'Did he see the father?'

Tension now, and the strain of gossip. The aunt took refuge in the cant, deferential, even obsequious to her companion. 'Just listen to what your mother will tell you. I know what she has suffered for all you children. You must listen to her now, for your own good.'

'Well, won't you tell me? Who was supposed to be the father?'

The mother braced herself for battle. This was the whole point now, the entire point of the midnight visit. 'He didn't say. But people have been telling me that you are going with a Northerner.'

The aunt interjected, 'It has made us all very unhappy.'

'Are men so short in town? Enh? Tell me Dehinwa, are good-looking, decent men so hard to find that you must go with a *Gambari*? Don't you know what your name is that you even let yourself be seen with a *Gambari*?'

'But mamma, you shouldn't listen to that kind of talk. Next time tell them to mind their business.'

The aunt left her mouth open in mid-swallow. 'What did the child say? Tell people to mind their own business when it is their love for your mother that prompts them to speak?'

'Who I move with is my own business.'

'Oh no, it isn't your own business, and you don't go with who you like, not if you are my own daughter. I should think I have a say in the matter. I haven't worked and slaved to send you to England and pulled strings to get you a really good post nearly in the Senior Service only to have you give me a Hausa grandson.'

'Mamma . . .'

'Well what did your father do? He didn't lift a finger to help you. He sent all his sons to England, but when it came to you, you remember what he said, don't you? But how could you? Sisi, better tell her what her father said. It was no secret, he repeated it all over town.'

The auntie nodded. 'He said he wasn't sending any girl to England only to go and get herself pregnant within three months.'

'His very words. I had only my petty trade, but from it I saved enough to send you on my own.'

Dehinwa bristled gradually. They had come to familiar grounds and now she was bored. 'All right, mamma, all right. I am saving as fast as I can. I'll pay you back what you spent on me before I ever get married.'

Tears now, tears for ingratitude, for toil and sacrifice unappreciated. Contrition, allowances, resuscitation of love and a little ground given. 'It isn't that I am even thinking of marriage or anything like that.' Always a mistake. 'Don't you see it is all in your own interest. We have no more

use for the world. God has spared us this long
only to look after you.'

The tone becomes lighter, everyone is crying
and blissfully unhappy. As once, months before,
at such a moment Dehinwa playfully said, 'But
really, mother, you mustn't make any more of
these midnight journeys. Suppose I had a man
with me?'

And the tears froze on the instant, and a slow
disbelief replaced the brief contentment. 'What
was that you said?' Anxious not to spoil things,
ready to sacrifice for the sake of peace, 'Come,
mamma, I was only joking.'

'I heard you. I heard what you said and you
were not joking. Suppose you had a man with
you? Enh, is that the sort of life you want to cut
out for yourself? God protect me, what sort of a
daughter have I born? If I found a man in your
house at any awkward hour I will let him know
that my family bears the name of Komolola. A
man in this house at night? I will cry *ibosi* on him
and humiliate him in public. . . .'

But tonight there was tact. By mutual consent
Sagoe did not exist, locked away like soiled linen
from decent sight. Only, the mother could not
quite forget and the aunt was slowly weighing up
the risks—did the mother wait for her to open up
that door? She was the whipping dog, but at such
times her function was nearly insupportable. Was
this a truce or was the battle to begin? She wiped
the bread-crumbs from the plate, avoiding the
mother's eyes. And Dehinwa, steeling herself for
the final act that must pronounce the break, was
slowly being worn down from the midnight visita-
tions of aunts and mothers bearing love, and

transparent intentions, and manufactured anxieties, and, quite simply, blood cruelty. . . .

Beautiful Feathers
Cyprian Ekwensi

When Wilson first met her, Yaniya was a glamorous young woman of nineteen, tall, hard-breasted and elegant, with a face sculptured out of Benin Bronzes, and descended directly from the famous Emotan whose statue dominates the city of Benin. Iyari was then a Government pharmacist, working from eight in the morning to two in the afternoon. Life was not unduly hectic, and she had all his attention. . . .

* * *

It was very much a Lagos courtship. Their parents were too far away to interfere. No one was present to ask questions about who slept where or with whom; Wilson did not seriously think of marrying her. But one morning he went to the hospital and they handed him an official letter. He was to proceed on transfer in fourteen days' time. Casually, he showed the note to Yaniya during the lunch break. She broke into tears. She vowed that if Wilson left her she would kill herself. In the evening her eyes were still swollen and the next day it was the same. The brightness had gone out

From *Beautiful Feathers*, © Cyprian Ekwensi, 1963. Reprinted by permission of Hutchinson Publishing Group, Ltd. and David Higham Associates, London.

of her life. She neglected her looks. Grief-stricken, she stared about her absently. He was confounded. Never could he once imagine that she had put her whole soul into the affair. He began to look at her with new eyes.

Yaniya had come to Lagos from Benin in search of work, and against her father's wish she had stayed on. She had not found it easy and, being beautiful, the men had wolfed her and left her heart-broken and faithless . . . but Wilson's kindness had again opened her heart. . . .

Wilson tried to nullify his own transfer so he could remain at headquarters in Lagos, near Yaniya. He failed. The medical authorities reminded him that Nigeria was one country. He must serve wherever he was posted. That determined him. He would take Yaniya along with him.

They had been living together for about three weeks now. She had given up her single room, selling her furniture and coming over in a suitcase-laden taxi. Since then the spinsterly hollows (so often misnamed 'slimness') had vanished from her cheeks, which now filled with a new radiance. The eager male-hunt look in her eye was now gone and in its place was a luminescent maturity nurtured by a love almost motherly. Yaniya was at the peak of her bloom. Wilson jocularly asked her, and she confessed: a baby was on the way. He decided immediately to marry her. She was overjoyed. . . .

Yaniya wanted to contribute something to the well-being of the new family so they could build together. She decided on a course in dressmaking, something she could practise while keeping house. She proved so adept with the needle that the Institute begged her specially to remain with them as an instructress. The wage was good and her hours of work did not unduly conflict with her one keen desire at the time: to look after Wilson. It was her big dream then. . . . One day she would take Wilson to Benin, she promised. She would show him to her father, and say, 'Did you not say I would never find happiness in Lagos?' One day.

Wilson in his courtship days did not see how extravagant she was. He did not see her fanatical devotion to clothes, lipstick, mascara, rouge, nail varnish and all the false apparatus of deceit so flagrantly misused by initiates to the art of glamour. He heard her tinny laughter, and it excited him then. He saw her attachment to the ephemerals of the city—garden parties, dances, football matches, purposeless meetings. . . . To him at the time it was a symbol of her 'sociableness.' . . .

* * *

Now there were three children and he could see things in a cold light. In his present position as leader of the Nigerian Movement for African and Malagasy Solidarity he could not afford to go through the scandal of a cleavage in his married life. Where did unity begin? He was sure she knew that, hence her new attitude. It would be a natural headline for a paper like the *West African Sensation*. The only way out of it all was to put up a placid front. He and Yaniya must still continue to be seen in public. They must smile and entertain, hold hands and say meaningless things for the benefit of the photographers and reporters, while underneath their hearts rotted with hate. This was the new Africa, deadly in its subtlety. . . .

* * *

He knew she had begun lately to be unfaithful to him. Who could the man be? A newcomer to

Lagos? It was such a big city she could begin with one of her former lovers and he would never know. Or was it some small irresponsible lad, a Grade Two clerk in some mercantile office whose entire salary could buy him only one pair of shoes? Women were unpredictable and stupid when it came to furtive affairs. With her three children, she might be fooling with a boy of nineteen for all he knew. Lagos was rapidly becoming Nigeria's divorce centre. It was the mark of its outward sophistication that nowhere did a happy marriage really exist. There was always the other man or the other woman. Marriage had become a sham, a facade, a social show-off. Once in a while husband and wife were seen together in public. Home life had vanished. The husband went on a mission to New York, taking with him a woman to warm his bed, the wife carried her typewriter and flew with policemen to the Congo. That was independence.

Daily he read the divorce cases. Up to this moment, he would never believe they were anything else but mere newspaper sensationalism: NURSING SISTER STEALS DOCTOR HUSBAND. HUSBAND SEES MAN KISSING WIFE IN GARAGE. WOMAN CLAIMS HEAVY DAMAGES IN MARRIAGE BREACH CASE. . . . They could never, in his imagination, involve real identifiable people with flesh and blood. If he was doing something about African Solidarity what was he doing about the disintegration of the Iyari family? His own children, members of his family, Lum, Pandhit, Jomo—they would soon grow up; into what? Disgruntled youths? . . .

She is going to meet her lover, Wilson thought. *I talk about solidarity. There it is! My own family split. But how can Africa be united when such a small unit as my family is not united?*

The Opportunity
Arthur Maimane

A room in Solomon's house—
the Lounge/Sitting-room.

EMMA: Solomon, why are you still sitting here so
late at night? You must come to sleep, my husband.

SOLOMON: (*dully*): Just now, Emma.

EMMA: It is three nights now that you do this.
What is the trouble?

SOLOMON: (*tired exasperation*): No trouble at
all, Emma. I'm just thinking.

EMMA: I know you too well, Solomon.

SOLOMON (*sighing*): Ah, sometimes one has to
make difficult decisions.

EMMA: If you know what is right and what is
wrong, then they are not so difficult to make.
You know that, Solly.

SOLOMON: Even if they hurt you?

EMMA: Do you mean hurt me? Or just the person
who makes them?

SOLOMON: You, them, me—anybody!

EMMA: If you know what is right, you make them.

SOLOMON: Like when the district commissioner
dismissed me from teaching because of politics?

EMMA: You helped to free our country, did you
not? Next month we shall be independent.

From *Ten One-Act Plays*, Cosmo Pieterse (ed.). Reprinted by permission of Heinemann Educational Books,
Ltd.

SOLOMON: You mean you were never angry with me even though for months I was unemployed?

EMMA: You were right, and I agreed with you.

SOLOMON: Because I was helping us to get independence? What would you say if I now told you that I must leave you because of this independence?

EMMA: Leave me? How leave me?

SOLOMON (*bitterly*): I mean divorce you!

EMMA: Solomon! How can you say such things? I am glad the children are sleeping and cannot hear you!

SOLOMON: I am serious, Emma. They want me to become an ambassador. To speak at the United Nations.

EMMA: That is a very important job, is it not?

SOLOMON (*extremely bitterly*): Oh, it is, Emma. Very! That is why they say I must divorce you. Because you are not educated.

EMMA: They think I will shame you?

SOLOMON: Yes.

EMMA: I would be lost in a place like that. It is somewhere in America, is it not?

SOLOMON: In New York.

EMMA (*thoughtfully*): Yes, in New York. Do you want to go?

SOLOMON: It is my big chance. If I refuse it— well, I don't know.

EMMA: You have done big things for our country.

SOLOMON: I have suffered for my country. Unemployment and even jail.

EMMA: Now it is my time to suffer.

SOLOMON (*with relieved surprise*): You agree then, Emma?

EMMA: No. I do not agree, Solomon. But you want to go. And I cannot go. My father and

mother gave me to you as a wife, so you must
do for me what you think is right.

SOLOMON: But I don't think this is right!

EMMA: But you want to go. I know you too well,
Solly. If you do not get what you want, there
will be no peace for you or for me. You will
make life unhappy for both of us.

SOLOMON: Oh, Emma, Emma! Am I that bad?
Why can't I pretend to you? Why couldn't I
pretend to be strong and decisive to you—I'm
sorry, Emma.

EMMA: Sorry? You forget that I was not born in
the town, Solly. I am a country woman, where
men are expected to make all the decisions.

SOLOMON: But what will the children say about a
divorce? Especially Monica?

EMMA: That one is worse than the white people,
I know. Too much education. Monica! My own
daughter, and most of the time I have no idea
how she thinks, or why?

SOLOMON: Yes, Monica. What is she going to say
when you—when we tell her?

EMMA (*ironically*): *You* must tell her. It is you
two who are educated, and *you* know how she
thinks. So you can tell her in a way that she will
understand.

SOLOMON: You are laughing at me now, Emma.
Don't you think—

EMMA: No, Solly. You must tell her. It is with
her that you must show what a strong man you
are in your mind. With me you can be easy and
tell me whatever you think. But with her you
must be strong. That way she will always respect you.

SOLOMON: Have I not been strong with her?

EMMA: Oh, you have been, my dear. But in the
way of the white man.

SOLOMON: D'you want me to put her over my knee and—

EMMA (*laughing*): That is not our only way, Solomon. You know that.

SOLOMON: Well, I'll talk to her. But I may need your help. So you must be there.

EMMA: Very well, Solomon. We'll do it tomorrow. But please come to bed now—it's so late.

The dining-room or the kitchen of Solomon's home. Next morning at breakfast. Wakey-wakey music on radio. Door opens and is banged shut.

MONICA (*cheerily*): Good morning, Papa. Good morning, Mama.

SOLOMON: Good morning, Monica.

EMMA (*scolding softly*): You must not always be late for breakfast, my child. Eating in a hurry is not good—

MONICA (*laughing easily*): I know, Mama. It's not good for your digestion! But then a good digestion means you put on weight—and that's the last thing I want to do.

EMMA: Ah, you modern girls. Figure, figure— that's all you think about. When I was a girl—

SOLOMON (*uneasily*): Is the modern girl going to be home early tonight?

MONICA: We-l-l, I don't know yet, Papa. Perhaps. It depends on what Joseph and I decide to do tonight. But I'll probably be home about—

EMMA (*motherly*): And how is Joseph, Monica? I have not seen him for a long time!

MONICA (*laughing with Solomon at an old family joke*): Oh, yes, we know, Mama! Three days can be a long time, when a loving mother like you is worrying if her daughter is ever going to get married. Oh, don't worry, Mama. Joseph will marry me any time I say so.

SOLOMON (*jokingly*): Isn't it for the poor boy to decide?

MONICA (*mock surprise*): Has any man ever done so, Papa? Eh, Mama? Doesn't he know yet that it is the women—

EMMA: Hush now, my child! That is not the way for children to talk.

MONICA (*some annoyance*): Oh, of course! Always a baby! Even if I'm grown up.

SOLOMON (*hurriedly*): I was asking if you're coming straight home because I—we want to talk to you, Monica. Something important.

MONICA (*after a brief, offended silence; grudgingly*): A family conference?

SOLOMON: Well, yes. I suppose you can call it that.

MONICA: What's it about?

SOLOMON: We'll tell you tonight, my girl.

MONICA (*a bit sharp*): The little girl treatment again!

SOLOMON: (*resignedly*): Well, it's about my new post in the government. After independence.

MONICA (*more friendly, with curiosity*): Are they going to give you a big job at last, Papa? What is it? They've already appointed all the ministers, and—

EMMA: Tonight, school teacher. You are getting late.

MONICA (*ironically*): That's right, Mama. Well, I'm off, people! See you tonight.

As for Scene Two. Same evening. Scene opens with closing of the BBC News.

SOLOMON: Hm, hm, that makes it ten past seven, and she isn't here yet.

MONICA (*cheerily*): Good evening, Mama, Papa! Here I am—almost on the dot!

EMMA: Hm. Did you see Joseph today?

MONICA (*laughing lightly*): Yes, Mama. And your son-in-law-to-be will be coming to see *you* later. When he comes to pick me up. Well, Papa? Here I am, ready to hear all the good news!

SOLOMON: It's good news and it's bad news too, my girl.

MONICA: How d'you mean, Papa?

SOLOMON (*clearing his throat*): Well, as you know, we're going to be independent very soon. Something we have fought for for a very long time. And independence means that we must have ambassadors who will represent their country—

MONICA (*excitedly*): Oh, Papa! Is that what you're going to be? I'm—

SOLOMON: Just wait a minute, my girl. Just listen quietly and understand everything I'm going to tell you. Remember I said it was good news and bad news too. (*Pause.*) Now, Monica, you're an educated girl—one of the best educated we have. *I* saw to that. So you will understand when I say that an ambassador—especially a senior one like I'm going to be—needs to have the kind of wife who can mix properly with the officials of foreign governments. Especially these imperialist governments, who don't really believe that we can rule ourselves. Is that not so?

MONICA (*slowly, after a pause*): Go on, Papa.

SOLOMON (*clearing his throat*): Your mother is not that kind of woman. She is not educated.

MONICA: So?

SOLOMON: So I will not get this posting if . . . if . . .

MONICA (*fiercely*): Go on!

EMMA (*speaking into the silence that follows*):
What he means, my child, is that he wants to
divorce me. And marry an educated girl.

MONICA: What! Is that true, Papa? You want to
—I can't believe it! I always thought you loved
Mama—

SOLOMON: What has love got to do with it?

MONICA: Everything! Love is the most important
thing in the world!

SOLOMON: That's your white man's education
talking, my girl. Respect! That is the important
thing! When your mother and I got married, respect was the thing that mattered.

MONICA: And now you don't respect her any
more? She can't read and write well enough for
an ambassador's wife?

SOLOMON: History is moving fast, and your
mother has been left behind.

MONICA: Do you agree to this, Mama?

EMMA: What is agree? What can I do? What can
any of us do? I must not stand in your father's
way, my child.

SOLOMON: I am glad to hear you speak like that,
Emma.

MONICA: Well, I'm not! I don't want to have divorced parents!

SOLOMON: I am doing it for our country.

MONICA: Our country! Is this 'country' thing more
important than the people who live in it? I say
to hell—

EMMA: Monica! Remember who you are talking
to!

MONICA: All right, I'm sorry I swore in front of
you. But tell me, what is this country if not us?
Tell me that!

SOLOMON (*quietly explanatory*): We are the
country—each single one of us. But the indi-

vidual is of no importance. It is only as a people
—as a nation—that we matter. Each *one* of us
is nothing without the others.

MONICA: I don't see these ministers we have be-
having like that. As far as they're concerned,
they're the only things that matter! Driving
around in their big, shiny cars as if—

EMMA: They are big and important men, my
child.

MONICA: And your husband is also going to become big and important? So he starts by driving
his big and shiny ambitions over you—over the
faithfulness, respect and everything you have
given him for more than a quarter of a century?
If that's the meaning of importance, I'm glad
I'm not important!

EMMA: Let your father speak, my child. I want to
understand him again.

MONICA: But what more can he say? He's said it
all! And you sit there quietly, saying there's
nothing you can do. Well, you can if you want
to! You can—

SOLOMON: Monica! You'd better stop right there!

MONICA: All right, Father. Tell us. Who *are* you
going to marry? Who is fit to be an ambassador's wife?

SOLOMON: We don't have to talk about that now.

EMMA: But you must tell her, Solomon. As our
eldest child she must know everything.

SOLOMON: Very well, you know her. Veronica.
The niece of the Minister of Education.

MONICA: What! That—that—

SOLOMON: Be very careful what you say about
her, Monica. She is going to be your *mother*
too, so you better start showing her some respect.

MONICA: She was my junior at secondary school

—and not a bright girl at all, from what I heard and saw of her. Veronica!

SOLOMON: It's probably just as well she's not as clever as you! Because you're so full of cheekiness and arguments!

MONICA: And she has accepted your proposal, Papa? Or wasn't that necessary? Is this to be *her* sacrifice to the nation? Her uncle, the minister, just tells you to marry her for the good of the nation and—snap—it's all arranged?

SOLOMON: She has accepted my proposal.

MONICA: You mean you just made an appointment for her to come to your office at party headquarters, popped the question and she said yes?

SOLOMON: Of course not!

MONICA: D'you realise what you're saying, Papa? You're implying that you have been having a love affair with this—this Veronica?

SOLOMON (*furious*): What business is that of yours? Eh?

MONICA: So it is true. Did you know about this, Mama?

EMMA: We always know these things, my child.

MONICA: And you accept it?

SOLOMON: What kind of a child did I bring to life? What has this education—(*Knock at the door.*) Who's that?

MONICA: I'll answer. I think it's Joe. I told you he was coming tonight. (*At door*) Hello, Joe. Come in.

JOSEPH: Hello, dear. (*Entering.*) Good evening, sir. Good evening, Mother. I hope you are both well tonight.

SOLOMON: Good evening, Joseph.

EMMA: Good evening, my son.

MONICA: None of us are *really* well tonight, Joe
—at least not in spirit.

SOLOMON: Be quiet, Monica!

MONICA: Quiet? But Joe is as good as one of the
family—what *was* a family, anyway. Don't you
think he has a right to know what's happening
to the family he's marrying into?

JOSEPH: I'm afraid I don't quite understand
what's going on . . .

EMMA: Would you like to have some tea, Joseph?

JOSEPH: Yes, Mother, please.

MONICA: Well, go on, Father. Tell Joseph what's
happened.

SOLOMON: I suppose you have heard, Joseph.
That I have been offered an ambassadorship?

JOSEPH: Yes, sir. And I was very pleased. But I
was not sure if it was time to congratulate you.

MONICA: It's not. It is a time for crying and the
gnashing of teeth. How can anybody ever make
such a demand of another man?

SOLOMON: It's not a demand, Monica.

MONICA: Tell me, Joe, d'you think it's right?

JOSEPH: What demand? I—I'm not sure I understand.

MONICA: Yes, you do! You're in the Prime Minister's office. Answer a simple question! Is it
right for your government to demand that my
father divorce my mother—just to become an
ambassador.

JOSEPH: Divorce! . . . Well, they want to send
him on a very important mission—

MONICA: The importance has nothing to do with
it! It's the principle that matters! I say it's im-
moral!

SOLOMON: But you're missing the whole point,
Monica.

EMMA: Here is the tea. I don't know what time we shall eat supper tonight with all this talk.

MONICA: You've come back just in time, Mama. Papa has finally come to the whole point. Go on, Papa.

SOLOMON: It's simple. I have explained the duties of an ambassador's wife, and it is quite obvious that she must be an educated woman.

MONICA: I see . . . d'you mean that even if they hadn't made the condition you'd still've divorced Mama to marry that girl?

SOLOMON (*sharp*): I didn't say that.

MONICA: But you mean that.

SOLOMON: Joseph, please explain the facts of life to this hot-headed idealist of yours!

JOSEPH: Well—I don't know how to say it, sir. All I think I can say is that your father's right, Monica. A senior ambassador, like he's going to be, needs an educated wife.

MONICA: And what about the Private Secretary to the Prime Minister? Am I educated enough for you, Joe? All I have is a B.A. you know.

JOSEPH (*laughing nervously*): You'll do. You're educated enough.

MONICA: Enough! Just as my mother was educated enough for my father twenty-seven years ago? But what's going to happen when they offer you a bigger job?

JOSEPH: I'm quite happy with my job.

MONICA: So was my father, twenty-seven years ago!

JOSEPH: You don't have to start quarrelling with me now, Monica.

MONICA: I'm not quarrelling . . .

EMMA (*interrupting*): Why don't we talk about

something else? It is not good to have hot talk
with your food. (*Turns to Joseph*) And how
have you been?

*Conversation and business ad lib during tea-
drinking. Emma clears table and begins to exit
with remains of cake etc.*

SOLOMON: Ah, that was very good tea, my dear.
And now I shall go and help you wash up. Will
you young people stay for supper, or are you
going out?

JOSEPH: Well, sir, we were planning to go—

MONICA: I don't think I want to go anywhere. I
couldn't face people tonight.

JOSEPH: All right.

SOLOMON (*going off—with tray of crockery; at a
distance*): Hold the door for me, Emma,
please.

JOSEPH: Whew! I didn't know I was going to walk
into anything like this, sweetheart.

MONICA: Would you've preferred not to be involved?

JOSEPH: Well, to tell you the truth, yes. I mean,
your father's an important person, and I
couldn't disagree with him and—

MONICA (*eagerly*): Then you think he's wrong?

JOSEPH: Well—don't let's jump to conclusions,
sweetheart. He was right on some things, but
not on others.

MONICA: I see . . . Even though you don't make
sense, I see.

JOSEPH: Oh, you're a bright girl, sweetheart. The
most intelligent girl in this country.

MONICA: Is that why you want to marry me?

JOSEPH: Well, that's got something to do with it.

MONICA: Would you still want to marry me if I was just an ordinary girl? Without a London University degree?

JOSEPH: How can I answer that? I've only known you as such a girl.

MONICA: But let's say you'd met me here, before I went to London?

JOSEPH: That's an unfair question, sweetheart.

MONICA: Oh, no, it's not! What do you love? Me or my education?

JOSEPH (*exasperated*): Monica, people are what they are because of their background. You have the personality I love, partly because of your education. I know I wouldn't love you if you were uneducated.

MONICA: So it is my education! Just like Papa married Mama because she could read and write! Today you love me because my education is good enough for you. But in ten years' time? He said Mama didn't keep up with him. What happens if I don't keep up with you? Will you also—

JOSEPH: None of us can look into the future, Monica.

MONICA: So! When we get married, you'll promise to love and protect me—till death do us part. But you won't mean any of it, will you? Because you can't foretell the future! You're a bright young man, Joseph—one of our very best. And though you say you can't foretell the future, you know it's going to be bright enough to fulfil your ambitions! And what about poor little me then? Eh? Tell me that!

JOSEPH (*light sarcasm*): If there's going to be any bright future in this country, you'll be there, Monica. I know you that well.

MONICA: Then you know me better than I know myself! I'm just a school teacher now, and I'm happy with it. I'm satisfied. I don't want to become a politician who places his country before his own family. All I want to be is a good wife to you and a good mother to our children. Like my mother! Oh yes! *I* am *proud* of my mother, if nobody else is! I want to be like her. So are you going to abandon me too when you have the chance to be a big shot who needs the other kind of a wife?

JOSEPH: I don't know what to say when you speak like that, Monica. All I can say is that I love you, and I want you to be my wife.

MONICA: And all I can say is that I'm not so sure if I still want to marry you. Perhaps I should look for a junior civil servant without your ambitions. You men of ambition! Who can trust you?

Door opens.

SOLOMON (*approaching*): Well, supper will be ready soon, my children! I'm sorry that you had to find us in the middle of such an embarrassing argument, Joseph, my son. But now everything is all right. The old woman and I finalised things in the kitchen.

JOSEPH: I'm glad to hear that, sir.

MONICA: And I'm glad for you too, Papa—though I'm sorry for you as well. And while you have been finalising things, we have been doing the opposite in here. We have broken things up.

JOSEPH (*pleading*): Oh Monica!

SOLOMON: What d'you mean by that?

MONICA: Oh, yes, Papa. There's going to be more

than one divorce in this family. At least I think
so. I haven't quite made up my mind yet. But
I'm thinking that I shouldn't make the same
mistake my mother made. Because Joe is ambitious like you, Papa. And you ambitious men
cannot be trusted. (*Solomon protests.*) At least
by unambitious women like me and my mother.
Veronica probably said she'd marry you because you were a big shot. Unlike the men of
her own age, who are still working their way up.
She's just the kind of wife you need to push you
and push you to the top.

SOLOMON (*interrupts*): But, Monica, you
don't . . . !

MONICA: But don't think you'll get there! Because the brilliant young men like Joe will already be waiting near the top—pushed up there
by their ambitious wives. And they'll kick you
in the teeth when you try and go past them to
the very top.

JOE (*interrupts*): How can you . . . ?

MONICA: I don't think I want to be involved when
that happens. So maybe I should disengage myself now, and leave the opportunities to you
great men of ambition!

SOLOMON: Monica!

JOSEPH: Monica, please!

MONICA: I don't think I want to see you again,
Joseph. Here's your ring . . . If you want me,
Papa, I shall be in the kitchen—with mother.

*Sharp exit. Momentary hush. Sobbing audible off;
soft consolatory noises . . .*

education

Through education we try to teach our children our own notion of civilization. African societies always had procedures for educating their young. They learned by working with their parents, by participating in community activities and by being initiated into adult responsibilities.

Western education was much less direct. It stressed the concepts of civilization rather than the experience of it. It became so intellectualized that it deceived itself into believing that all civilization was Western. Then it propagated this false notion to people in the non-Western world and actually taught them that they were uncivilized. It built Western-type schools to teach African children about the West, completely ignoring African civilization in the process.

Now a reorientation of African education has begun. But only a few years ago, a Ghanaian teacher of teen-age boys, Joseph Abruquah, reminisced: "The task of Grammar School was to transform bush boys into civilized men." Those students got the impression that civilization was an *iron brush to straighten hair, Asepso soap to bleach the face, supper without red pepper and a toothbrush with Pepsodent!*

A popular understanding of civilization in the West is that it is a condition of human society marked by an advanced stage of development in the arts and sciences and by corresponding social, political and cultural complexity, and therefore superior to all other modes of human society.

If complexity is the essence of civilization, the West's civilization is superior to Africa's. If advancement of spirituality commensurate with advancement of technology is the essence of civilization, it is not clear who is ahead. Perhaps the essence of civilization is a frame of mind, a mental set, that appreciates the relativity of revelation— being willing to hold different points of view in one's head at the same time and consider the truth in each. Perhaps the essence of civilization is a quality of the human spirit that shows concern for the personhood of all mankind. No part of the world has a monopoly on these "civilizing processes." Every place in the world is in great need of more.

Four writers describe schooling in their four corners of Africa. In Tell Freedom, Peter Abrahams, a colored South African, narrates his own first-grade experience with an Afrikaner principal whom most whites consider "mad" because he cares about colored children. Mr. Visser immediately observes the great potential in Peter and seeks to develop his personhood.

In Weep Not, Child, James Ngugi of Kenya tells about a prestigious mission preparatory school for African boys. The principal in this story is a white British missionary who believes *white ways are superior though he is eager to share this superiority with blacks. This principal has not yet grasped the "relativity of all truth." He is also unable to see that he is an arm of a racist government during the war taking place in the story. White settlers always called it Mau Mau to imply that Kikuyus were barbarians who considered murder to be moral. White settlers never pointed out that 15,000 black Kenyans were killed in the war, but only 35 white Europeans were killed.*

Important people in this story are Mr. Howlands, a white settler, and Stephen, his teen-age son; Mwihaki, the girl Njoroge loves, and her father, Jacobo, a black quisling who supports Howlands for personal profit; Njeri and Nyokabi are Njoroge's mothers in this polygamous Kikuyu family.

In America, Their America, *J. P. Clark writes about his year's stay in the U.S.A. during the early sixties. He had already graduated from the University of Ibadan in Nigeria and published poems and plays before he came West. As an entirely urbane young man, he enjoys driving home his point that the U.S.A. does not have a corner on civilization. In fact he relishes repeating that Nigerian civilization is vastly superior.*

In I Will Try, *Legson Kayira of Malawi presents a simpler account of elementary and high school education near his home village in Malawi, and of his need to leave his nation in search of a university. So he starts to walk to America. In this writer's view neither his Central African culture nor his adopted American culture contain all there is of civilization. One needs to be a citizen of both, a citizen of the world.*

Tell Freedom
Peter Abrahams

One lunch-time, after I had cleaned his car,
Mr. Wylie said:

'There are some sandwiches on my desk. Take
them.'

He drove off. I went to the office. The short-
sighted Jewish girl was in her corner, eating her
lunch and reading. She looked up.

'Mr. Wylie said I can have that.' I pointed.

'All right.'

I took the little package and turned to the door.

'Lee.'

I stopped and turned to her.

'That is your name, isn't it?'

'Yes, missus.'

'Miss, not missus. You only say missus to a
married woman.'

Her smile encouraged me.

'We say it to all white women.'

'Then you are wrong. Say miss.'

'Yes, miss.'

'That's better. . . . Tell me, how old are you?'

'Going on for eleven, miss.'

'Why don't you go to school?'

'I don't know, miss.'

From *Tell Freedom*, © Peter Abrahams. Reprinted by
permission of Alfred A. Knopf, Inc., New York.

'Don't you want to?'

'I don't know, miss.'

'Can you read or write?'

'No, miss.'

'Stop saying miss now.'

'Yes, miss.'

She laughed.

'Sit down. Eat your sandwiches if you like.'

I sat on the edge of the chair near the door.

'So you can't read?'

'No, miss.'

'Wouldn't you like to?'

'I don't know, miss.'

'Want to find out?'

'Yes, miss.'

She turned the pages of the book in front of her. She looked at me, then began to read from *Lamb's Tales from Shakespeare*.

The story of Othello jumped at me and invaded my heart and mind as the young woman read. I was transported to the land where the brave Moor lived and loved and destroyed his love.

The young woman finished.

'Like it?'

'Oh yes!'

'Good. This book is full of stories like that. If you go to school you'll be able to read them for yourself.'

'But can I find a book like that?'

'Yes. There are many books.'

'The same one with the same story?'

'There are thousands.'

'Exactly like it?'

'Exactly.'

'Then I'm going to school!' . . .

* * *

'All right. You may sit down. This is our new boy, Peter Abrahams. Make room for him in the corner at the back, Adams.'

'Please, miss . . .'

'Yes?'

'There is no room. We're so tight we can hardly move our arms to write.'

'Peter must have a place. Make room as best you can.'

'Yes, miss.'

'Now! Put up your hands those of you who have whole slates. Not one?'

'They're all cracked, miss.'

'It doesn't matter if they are cracked. Up now . . . One . . . Two. Only three?' . . .

'Please, miss . . .'

'Yes, Thomas?'

'My slate is cracked across the middle. I can let him . . .'

'Peter.'

'That is very good of you, Thomas. Thank you. But isn't that where Jones sits? He'll be back to-morrow and want his seat.'

'He's not coming back, miss. His father's gone to jail so he must go to work to help his mother.'

'Are you sure of this?'

'Yes, miss.'

'It's a shame. You liked Jones so much, didn't you, miss?'

'That's enough out of you, Adams. Thank you, Thomas.'

'Is your father alive, Peter?'

'No, miss.'

'Then things are not too easy?'

'No, miss.'

'Take this card. You'll see children standing in a line during the lunch break. Join them and show this and you'll get a free lunch. That's all. You can go to your place.'

'Thank you, miss. I'm sorry to make more work for you.'

'Come back here, Peter. . . . I don't want you to think any more about making work for me or anybody. Understand?'

'Yes, miss.'

'We are here to teach and help you. I'm sorry I made you think that. You've often said something you don't mean, haven't you?'

'Yes, miss.'

'Well, it was the same. Don't think about it. And don't repeat what you heard me and the other teacher say about the Principal.'

'Yes, miss.'

* * *

A B C D E F G,
H I J K L M N,
O P Q R S T U,
V W X Y Z makes the Alpha-bet . . .

* * *

'Please, miss . . .'

'Yes?'

'Are all the books in the world made from the alphabet?'

'Yes, all the books in the world are made from the alphabet.'

'Jee-zus!'

'What?'

'Nothing, miss; thank you.'

'Hey! Look at the new one among our hungry

lot. He's in our class. Peter Abrahams. Hey! Peter
Abrahams! Like lining up with the other cattle
for a bit of bread and dirty cocoa? They spit in
the cocoa!'

'Ha! ha! ha! ha!'

* * *

'Hey! No use running away, you little coward!
I know you! Come here!'

'Sir?'

'I heard what you said. I've a good mind to
expel you!'

'Didn't mean anything, sir.'

'Of course not! That's the trouble with you and
this country and all of us. We don't mean anything. You're looked down upon. Have you learnt
nothing from it? Must you look down on someone
else? Go away! If I hear any more remarks from
you or anyone else. . . . Teacher!'

'Sir?'

'Is there no way we can protect these children
from the vulgar remarks of others while they get
their food?'

'No, sir.'

'They're being humiliated for being poorer than
their fellows. Snobbery among the op-
pressed!' . . .

* * *

'Ah, Abrahams. So you're letting things slip
after only six months.'

'No, sir.'

'Are you calling the teacher a liar?'

'No, sir.'

'Are you tired of working hard? Letting me
down? None of the others have, you know. Do you
want to do only the ordinary classes?'

'No, sir.'

'You'd better tell me all about it.'

'It's arithmetic, sir.'

'What about it?'

'I can't do it, sir.'

'Have you tried?'

'Yes, sir.'

'Hard?'

'Yes, sir.'

'This record says you show no real interest in it.'

'I've tried, sir.'

'Do you mean the record is untrue?'

'No, sir. I mean I've tried hard to be interested.'

'And failed?'

'Yes, sir.'

'You know, of course, that I don't make the laws about examinations.'

'Yes, sir.'

'Well, unless you get a certain average for arithmetic your very high average in all the other subjects won't help you. That is the law, and I didn't make it. I want to push you through as fast as I can but you must work at arithmetic. Relax a little with the other subjects, if you like.'

'I like the other subjects, sir.'

'I know. But to get where you want to go you can't only do what you like . . . Where do you want to go? What do you want to do?

'Those stories, sir.'

'In the book the young woman gave you?'

'Yes, sir.'

'I was wondering whether you had begun to forget them.'

'I'm trying to read it now, sir.'

'Getting anything out of it?'

'A little.'

"Well, there you have it. Between you and the further knowledge that would help you get everything out of that book, stands arithmetic. It's like a lion barring your road. You either turn back because you cannot cope with it, or you kill it, and go on. There is no other way. The makers of our educational laws have not provided for poets. I want you to kill that lion and go on. Arithmetic is silly in a poet's armoury but you must master it and get that average. . . . I promised you my cane if you were ever sent to me. We must keep our promises. Let down your trousers, then go back and let the sting of the cane help you kill the lion. . . .'

* * *

'Hello, Peter.'

'Hello, Ellen.'

'Walk with me to the end of the playground.'

'I can't.'

'Please . . . Or don't you want to?'

'I want to but I can't.'

'Why not?'

'Why do you ask me when you know I have to line up?'

'Please don't be angry.'

'Then don't ask when you know the answer.'

'I only asked because you don't have to line up.'

'I want to eat.'

'I brought an extra lunch.'

'For me?'

'Yes.'

'Why?'

'I like you. You're the best boy in Visser's special.'

'Arendse gets better marks.'

'Only in the things you don't like.'

'His average is better.'

'I heard a teacher say your intelligence was better. And I agree. Come. I'm shy. I don't want to give you your lunch where everybody can see.'

'I thought you were poorer than me. You are thinner.'

'We're poor in everything except food. My ma works where they waste a lot of food and she brings a lot of it home. There's chicken in your sandwiches. I can't get fat no matter how much I eat. Suppose I'd better tell you I've got a bad chest.'

'Why?'

'Here, take your sandwiches. We're far away from the others now. Let's go'n sit under that tree . . . Nice?'

'Hmmm.'

'I'm glad. I'll bring you all the nicest things. I've some sweets for after.'

'I've nothing to give you.'

'I don't want anything. I just want you to be my boy if you like me. That's why I told you about my chest. My granny says one must always tell the truth. But even if you don't like me, I will still bring your lunch every day. What I mean is every day as long as my ma stays with us. She may go away and then there won't be any more food. . . . Do you like me?'

'Yes.'

'Really? Cross your heart?'

'Cross my heart.'

'I thought you did, but I wasn't sure. But I knew you'd never tell me if I didn't ask you. And it's not easy for a girl to tell a boy she likes him.'

'It's not easy for a boy.'

'Not if he's like you. . . . Have some of mine,

please. I can't eat all of it. And a man must eat more than a woman. I told my granny all about you. She wants me to bring you home. But you must not come if you don't want to.'

'I want to! I'll carry your books this afternoon.'

'Good. Oh, I'm so glad you won't be in the line-up again. It made me want to cry when I heard them say things.'

'Wish I could give you something. Here, I've a top and some marbles.'

'Keep them . . . Just be my boy.'

'I am your boy and I think you're the nicest girl in the school.'

'I'm dark and I have kinky hair.'

'Who cares? I like you!'

'I want you to top the class for me!'

'No. you must be first. That's what I want. Will you?'

'I'll try if that's what you really want.'

'You'll be first, I'll be second and old Arendse third. I want to be proud of my girl.'

'All right! I'll do it. . . . There's the bell. Golly, we'll have to run. We'll be late.'

'Give me your hand.'

'Not too fast, please. It'll make me cough.'

Weep Not, Child
James Ngugi

Conditions went from bad to worse. No one could tell when he might be arrested for breaking

From *Weep Not, Child,* © James Ngugi, 1964, Reprinted by permission of Heinemann Educational Books, Ltd.

the curfew. You could not even move across the courtyard at night. Fires were put out early for fear that any light would attract the attention of those who might be lurking outside. It was said that some European soldiers were catching people at night, and having taken them to the forest would release them and ask them to find their way back home. But when their backs were turned they would be shot dead in cold blood. The next day this would be announced as a victory over Mau Mau. . . .

* * *

Mr. Howlands felt a certain gratifying pleasure. The machine he had set in motion was working. The blacks were destroying the blacks. They would destroy themselves to the end. What did it matter with him if the blacks in the forest destroyed a whole village? What indeed did it matter except for the fact that labour would diminish? Let them destroy themselves. Let them fight against each other. The few who remained would be satisfied with the land the white man had preserved for them. Yes, Mr. Howlands was coming to enjoy his work. At the beginning of the emergency, when he had been called from the farm, he had been angry. He had at times longed to go back to the life of a farmer. But as the years went, the assertive desire to reduce to obedience had conquered, enabling him to do his work with a thoroughness that would not have been possible with many of his age. . . .

* * *

Siriana Secondary School was a well-known centre of learning. Being one of the earliest schools to be started in the colony, it had expanded much due mainly to the efforts of its missionary founders.

To Njoroge, coming here was nearly the realization of his dreams. He would for the first time be taught by white men. And this was what confused him. Though he had never come into real contact with white men, yet if one had met him and had abused him or tried to put him in his place, Njoroge would have understood. He would have even known how to react. But not when he met some who could smile and laugh. Not when he met some who made friends with him and tried to help him in his Christian progress.

Here again, he met boys from many tribes. Again if these had met him and had tried to practise dangerous witchcraft on him, he would have understood. But instead he met boys who were like him in every way. He made friends and worked with Nandi, Luo, Wakamba, and Giriama. They were boys who had hopes and fears, loves and hatreds. If he quarrelled with any or if he hated any, he did so as he would have done with any other boy from his village.

The school itself was an abode of peace in a turbulent country. Here it was possible to meet with God, not only in the cool shelter of the chapel, where he spent many hours, but also in the quietness of the library. For the first time he felt he would escape the watchful eyes of misery and hardship that had for a long time stared at him in his home. Here he would organize his thoughts and make definite plans for the future. He was sure that with patience and hard work, his desire to have learning would be fulfilled. Maybe the sun would soon rise to announce a new day.

Siriana Secondary School took part in inter-school sports meetings at which some Asian and European schools took part. The Hill School was a famous school for European boys.

The Hill School sent a team of boys to Siriana for football. It was four o'clock. Along with the eleven players were some who were mere specta-tors. Njoroge did not play football and it hap-pened that he fell into conversation with one of the visitors not actively engaged in playing. But as soon as Njoroge spoke to the boy, he felt that he must have seen him somewhere else. The boy was tall, with long brown hair that kept on being blown on to his face by the wind. He had to keep on swinging his head to make the threads of hair return to their proper places.

'I think I've seen you before,' Njoroge at last said as he took the boy round.

'Have you?' The boy looked up at Njoroge full in the eyes. At first he seemed puzzled. Then his face brightened up. He said, 'Oh, do you come from Kipanga?'

'Yes. That's where I've seen you before.'

'I remember. You are the son of Ngotho who —' The boy suddenly stopped.

'My name is Stephen. Stephen Howlands.'

'I am Njoroge.'

They walked on in silence. Njoroge saw he was not afraid of Stephen. Here in school, Stephen was a boy. Njoroge could not be afraid of a boy.

'When did you come here?'

'At the beginning of this year. And you?'

'Been in Hill School for two years.'

'Which school did you go to before you came here?'

'Nairobi. What about you?'

'I went to Kamahou Intermediate School.'

'Is that the school you went to when you passed near our home?'

'No. That one was Kamae Primary School and went up to Standard IV. Did you see me?'

'Yes.' Stephen could easily recall the many times he had hidden in the hedge near his home with the object of speaking to Njoroge or any other of the children. Yet whenever they came near he felt afraid.

'We didn't see you.'

'I used to hide near the road. I wanted to speak with some of you.' Stephen was losing his shyness.

'Why didn't you?'

'I was afraid.'

'Afraid?'

'Yes. I was afraid that you might not speak to me or you might not need my company.'

'Was it all that bad?'

'Not so much.' He did not want sympathy.

'I am sorry I ran away from you. I too was afraid.'

'Afraid?' It was Stephen's turn to wonder.

'Yes. I too was afraid of you.'

'But I meant no harm.'

'All the same I was. How could I tell what you meant do do?'

'Strange.'

'Yes. It's strange. It's strange how you do fear something because your heart is already prepared to fear because maybe you were brought up to fear that something, or simply because you found others fearing. . . . That's how it's with me. When my brothers went to Nairobi and walked in the streets, they came home and said that they didn't like the way Europeans looked at them.'

'I suppose it's the same everywhere. I have heard many friends say they didn't like the way Africans looked at them. And when you are walking in Nairobi or in the country, though the sky may be clear and the sun is smiling, you are still not free to enjoy the friendliness of the sky because you are aware of an electric tension in the air. . . . You cannot touch it, you cannot see it . . . but you are aware of it all the time.'

'Yes. Till sometimes it can be maddening. You are afraid of it and if you try to run away from it, you know it's all futile because wherever you go it's there before you.'

'It's bad.'

'It's bad,' agreed Njoroge. They felt close together, united by a common experience of insecurity and fear no one could escape.

'Yet the country is so cool and so absorbing. . . .'

'It's a land of sunshine and rain and wind, mountains and valleys and plains. Oh—but the sunshine—'

'But so dark now.'

'Yes—so dark, but things will be all right.'

Njoroge still believed in the future. Hope of a better day was the only comfort he could give to a weeping child. He did not know that this faith in the future could be a form of escape from the reality of the present.

The two had moved away from the crowd and were standing together under a black wattle tree.

'I'll be away from home soon.'

'Where will you go?'

'To England.'

'But that's your home?'

'No. It isn't. I was born here and I have never
been to England. I don't even want to go there.'

'Do you have to go?

'Yes. Father did not want to, but my mother
wanted us to go.'

'When will you go?'

'Next month.'

'I hope you'll come back?'

A wave of pity for this young man who had to
do what he did not want to do filled Njoroge.
At least, he, Njoroge, would rise and fall with his
country. He had nowhere else to go.

'I want to come back.'

'Is your father going with you?'

'No. He'll remain here. But—but—you sometimes get a feeling that you're going away from
someone forever. . . . That's how I feel and
that's what makes it all so awful.'

Again silence settled between them. Njoroge
wanted to change the subject.

'They have changed sides.'

'Let's go and cheer.'

The two moved back to the field, again shy
with each other. They moved into two different
directions as if they were afraid of another contact.

* * *

It was a cold Monday morning. Njoroge had
gone through the first two terms and now was in
the third. It would soon end. Njoroge woke up as
usual, said his prayers and prepared himself for
the morning parade. It was such a pleasant morning in spite of the cold. After the roll call he went
to the chapel for a communion with God, and
then to the dining hall for breakfast; that was al-

ways the daily routine. He ate his breakfast quickly for he had not yet finished the preparation for the previous night.

The first class was English. Njoroge loved English literature.

'Why, you look happy today,' a boy teased him.

'But I'm always happy,' he said.

'Not when we're doing maths,' another boy put in.

They laughed. Njoroge's laughter rang in the class. The first boy who had spoken said, 'See, see how he's laughing. He is happy because this is an English class.'

'Do you want me to cry?' Njoroge asked. He felt buoyant.

'No. It's only that my mother tells me that a man should not be too happy in the morning. It's an ill-omen.'

'Don't be superstitious.'

Yet Njoroge did not like the last observation. All through the week that had passed, he had been assailed by bad dreams. The dreams had affected him so much that he had been unable to write to Mwihaki. Tonight, however, he would write to her. He wanted to tell her that Stephen had gone back to England and his sister had accompanied them. She would however come back to continue her missionary work. When he first met Stephen he had written to her, telling her about his own impression of Stephen. 'He looked lonely and sad' he had finished.

There was a lot of shouting in the room. Then one boy whispered: 'Teacher. Hush!' There was silence in the room. The teacher came in. He was always on time. Njoroge was often surprised by

these missionaries' apparent devotion to their
work. One might have thought that teaching was
to them life and death. Yet they were white men.
They never talked of colour; they never talked
down to Africans; and they could work closely,
joke, and laugh with their black colleagues who
came from different tribes. Njoroge at times
wished the whole country was like this. This
seemed a little paradise, a paradise where children
from all walks of life and of different religious
faiths could work together without any consciousness. Many people believed the harmony in the
school came because the headmaster was a strange
man who was severe with everyone, black and
white alike. If he was quick to praise what was
good, he was equally quick to suppress what he
thought was evil. He tried to bring out the good
qualities in all, making them work for the good
name of the school. But he believed that the best,
the really excellent could only come from the
white man. He brought up his boys to copy and
cherish the white man's civilization as the only
hope of mankind and especially of the black races.
He was automatically against all black politicians
who in any way made people to be discontented
with the white man's rule and civilizing mission.

Njoroge was in the middle of answering a question when the headmaster came to the door. The
teacher went out to see what the headmaster
wanted. When he came back, he loooked at
Njoroge and told him that he was wanted outside.

His heart beat hard. He did not know what the
headmaster could have to say to him. A black car
stood outside the office. But it was only when
Njoroge entered the office and saw two police

officers that he knew that the car outside had something to do with him. Njoroge's heart pounded with fear.

The headmaster said something to the two officers who immediately withdrew.

'Sit down, my boy.' Njoroge, whose knees had already failed him, gladly sank into the chair. The headmaster looked at him with compassionate eyes. He continued, 'I'm sorry to hear this about your family.'

Njoroge watched the missionary's face and lips. His own face did not change but Njoroge listened keenly with clenched teeth.

'You're wanted at home. It's a sad business . . . but whatever your family may have made you do or take in the past, remember Christ is there at the door, knocking, waiting to be admitted. That's the path we've tried to make you follow. We hope you'll not disappoint us.' The headmaster sounded as if he would cry.

But when Njoroge went to the car he realized that the headmaster had not given him a clue as to what his family had done. His words of comfort had only served to increase Njoroge's torment.

He would never forget his experience in the post. That particular homeguard post was popularly known as the House of Pain. The day following his arrival in the post he was called in to a small room. Two European officers were present. One had a red beard.

'What's your name?' the red beard asked, while the grey eyes looked at him ferociously.

'Njo-ro-ge.'

'How old are you?'

'I think 19 or thereabouts.'

'Sema affande!' one of the homeguards outside the small room shouted.

'Affande.'

'Have you taken the Oath?'

'No!'

'Sema affende!' barked the same homeguard.

'No Affendi.'

'How many have you taken?'

'I said none affendi!'

The blow was swift. It blinded him so that he saw darkness. He had not seen the grey eyes rise.

'Have you taken Oath?'

'I-am-a-school-boy-affendi,' he said, automatically lifting his hands to the face.

'How many Oaths have you taken?'

'None, sir.'

Another blow. Tears rolled down his cheeks in spite of himself. He remembered the serenity of his school. It was a lost paradise.

'Do you know Boro?'

'He's my—brother—'

'Where is he?'

'I—don't—know—'

Njoroge lay on the dusty floor. The face of the grey eyes had turned red. He never once spoke except to call him Bloody Mau Mau. A few seconds later Njoroge was taken out by the two homeguards at the door. He was senseless. He was covered with blood where the hob-nailed shoes of the grey eyes had done their work.

He woke up from the coma late in the night. He heard a woman screaming in a hut not far from the one in which he lay. Could it be Njeri? Or Nyokabi? He shuddered to think about it. He longed to see them all once again before he died.

For he thought this was the end. Perhaps death
was not bad at all. It sent you into a big sleep
from which you never awoke to the living fears,
the dying hopes, the lost visions.

They had not finished with him. He was in the
room the next day. What would he do if they
asked him the same questions again? Tell a lie?
Would they leave him alone if he said yes to every
question? He doubted it. His body had swollen all
over. But the worst thing for him was the fact he
was still in the dark about all this affair.

'You are Njoroge?'

'Yees.'

'Have you taken Oath?' All eyes turned to him.
Njoroge hesitated for a moment. He noticed that
Mr. Howlands was also present. The grey eyes
took the momentary hesitation and said, 'Mark,
you tell us the truth. If you tell the truth, we shall
let you go.' The pain in his body came and asked
him to say *Yes*. But he instinctively said *No* with-
drawing a few steps to the door. Nobody touched
him.

'Who murdered Jacobo?' Mr. Howlands asked
for the first time. For a time, Njoroge was shaken
all over. He thought he was going to be sick.

'Murdered?' he hoarsely whispered in utter un-
belief. And all of a sudden a strong desire to know
if Mwihaki was safe caught him. He for a moment
forgot that he was addressing his enemies.

The white men closely watched him.

'Yes. Murdered.'

'By whom?'

'You'll tell us that.'

'Me, Sir? But—'

'Yes. You'll tell us.'

Mr. Howlands rose and came to Njoroge. He

was terrible to look at. He said, 'I'll show you.' He held Njoroge's private parts with a pair of pincers and started to press tentatively.

'You'll be castrated like your father.'

Njoroge screamed.

'Tell us. Who really sent you to collect information in Jacobo's house about . . .?'

Njoroge could not hear: the pain was so bad. And yet the man was speaking. And whenever he asked a question, he pressed harder.

'You know your father says he murdered Jacobo.'

He still screamed. Mr. Howlands watched him. Then he saw the boy raise his eyes and arms as if in supplication before he became limp and collapsed on the ground. Mr. Howlands looked down on the boy and then at the officers and walked out. The red beard and the grey eyes laughed derisively.

Njoroge was not touched again and when he became well a few days later, he and his two mothers were released.

America, Their America
J. P. Clark

'You sure have a big chip on your shoulder!' I was often admonished by Americans, not least by the most unprivileged of them.

Being undilutedly black, and coming from a so-

From *America, Their America*, © 1964 by J. P. Clark. Reprinted by permission of André Deutsch, Ltd., London.

called undeveloped country and continent, I confess I must have felt and probably shall remain
bitter at and jealous of all that passes and sells so
loudly as western and white civilization, achieved
as likely as not at the expense of the dark. And
this was so with me going through Europe and
England; America, my destination, just happened
to be the limit, both of the dream and of the
actuality of that achievement crying pride and
power everywhere. . . .

Undoubtedly, I proved myself a most awkward
guest. . . .

At nearly all the large house parties I had in-
vitations to, either from couples living in a per-
petual state of unpack in tenement buildings, say
in the deep lower and upper reaches of New York,
or from career couples comfortably established in
shiny, anonymous apartment blocks, as well as
from upper middle class, middle-aged couples retired far from the madding crowd in wooden-
fronted suburban mansions, I always ended up
right in the heart of a curious circle of guests asking this or that question about Africa and giving
me that knowing quizzical look when I provided a
piece of information quite contrary to the proto-
type image they had in mind. The tenement people showed a preference for the arty subjects and
were more open and disinterested in discussing
matters American.

On the other hand, the aspiring prospering professionals inclined to topics political or economics
and sociology within their group. Conversation
was often a criss-cross of comparisons and queries
to the ding-dong tune of 'did-you-read-that?'
and 'you-should-read-the-other-fellow: his-latest-
work-is-a-sure-must.' With the propertied and the
nouveau riche, usually ensconced away in self-

contained communities, the pattern becomes even
more interesting. First one accommodating man,
armed with a glass of gin or some other firewater,
ambles up and discloses a mind curious for geog-
raphy. He takes a chair by me in one corner of the
overdone and decorated lounge, and immediately
another pulls up his seat to join in so that before
we have left the realm of the flora and fauna of
Africa, others have made a complete circle about
us. How is the state of education down there?
Nigeria has up to five colleges? Always thought
the place no bigger than a penny-stamp on the
map. And you have cities and civilizations long established before Columbus discovered us? Fancy
that! Now, which of the presidents was shot recently? Oh, yes, aren't things a bit unstable there
right now? You don't think so? In other words,
you are saying foreign investment would be safe
for a long time to come in the New Africa. Hm,
the newspapers don't make it look so!

But the discussion, somewhat dry and imper-
sonal before, inevitably turns to sex, love and
marriage habits in other lands, that is, in Africa,
as compared to the honourable, democratic practice of co-equal, loving partners observed among
American couples. By this time however, the
ladies in their silk and fineries, smelling a con-
spiracy of males against their dominance of the
house, fan their way floatingly to form an outer
ring to the group. Did they understand me to be
offering defence for the obnoxious practice of
polygamy. . . .

'Still I don't see how I can share one man with
another woman—Darling, that would be like al-
lowing you other lovers!'

The women remain petulant together.

'Well, the fellow says his mother is quite happy with his father who has a dozen other wives,' the darling husbands assure them.

'O la la!' issues the universal whistle.

'And no two persons could be closer than my mother and father are,' I rub it in.

'How can that be?' The women rise in one voice.

'One man to several women deprives the wife of her rights!' they intone together.

'And what are those rights?' I laugh.

Surprisingly, there is a hush, for none there can think up immediately their famous well guaranteed rights. Until one, spirited and aloud, speaks of her co-equal rights to any property her husband has—like the home and his business. To this I say my mother has her self-contained apartment in the concession or compound and that she has her own farming, fishing, or independent trading to do when not helping with the larger business of the husband. And at her age, which probably is that of many of my fellow guests, she would be too concerned with the well-being of her children to go nervous and neurotic over sex as apparently is the preoccupation of most American wives.

'Oh, that's not fair at all,' come the protests, frantic still but becoming decidedly abashed. . . .

'And I still think polygamy an obnoxious practice.'

'Oh, not so different from what the young man calls our serial system of marrying today only to divorce tomorrow to begin a long string of uncertain couplings.'

'That at least is a democratic process, and things are even between both parties.'

So ran the conversation at a typical big bour-

geois house party I attended, everybody talking at
the same time, not to advance the progress of anything but usually only so that each could score a
point and not feel left out and without really having to listen to one another. The gentleman who
had started it all with me earlier in the evening
rose up at last to go home. 'Young man,' he held
my hand, 'let me know when you are returning
home. I sure want a holiday in Africa.'

I Will Try
Legson Kayira

NYASALAND

Toward the end of my stay at Livingstonia, we
had often read of students from Uganda and
Kenya who went to the United States for their
college work. . . . I would go to the United
States, I decided. . . .

I was going to get jobs on the way. . . . I had
rushingly said that I would leave on Tuesday,
October 14, 1958, and there was no changing if I
wanted to leave.

That evening I overheard an interesting speech
by my mother. She was standing outside our
house, all alone, and she was talking. I listened,
and she was mentioning my father's name and

From the book *I Will Try* by Legson Kayira. Copyright
© 1965 by Legson Kayira. Reprinted by permission of
Doubleday & Company, Inc.

many other names that I had never heard of before. "Your child is going away," she said. "Give him good luck. Drive away the danger from him. Give him wisdom to return home." . . .

It was that morning of October 14 in the year of 1958. It was that day I had scheduled myself to pull myself from this routine of which I was a part, to pull myself out of it, and yet sincerely hope and pray that someday I would return to it and hope it would welcome me back as a full part. . . .

It was mid-morning when I was ready to leave. "Wherever you go," my mother said, "I shall always recognize your footprints." . . . She handed me my white bag containing flour for the five-day trip to the United States of America, an extra khaki shirt, a blanket, and the two books, the English Holy Bible and the *Pilgrim's Progress*. In my left hand I was holding an axe, my axe. My father had made it for me when I was still a child going to Mpale Village School. I was going to take it along.

UGANDA

On January 19 in the year of our Lord one thousand nine hundred and sixty, I arrived in Kampala, a vast and impressive commercial city in the Protectorate of Uganda. . . .

During one of the days that I spent looking for a job, I had occasion to wander into the city. While there I happened to bump into the British Consul Library, which was adjacent to what I was later told was the Legislative Chambers. Now that I had discovered a library I would have to come here whenever I was free, especially since I was not permitted to borrow any books since I was not

a member and since it required payment of a
certain fee to be a member. I was not charged
anything for reading in the library. . . .

During this time I began frequenting the British
Consul Library whenever I was free. I would walk
the five miles to the city, spend a few hours reading in the library, then go back to the house. One
February morning I was hurrying to mail a letter
home, and I had hoped I would, after attending to
the duty of my letter, stop at the library and
browse a little bit before returning to the house.
On the way I was joined by a young man. . . .

"Haven't I seen you somewhere around here?"

"I don't know." . . .

"Let me see," he began, "were you not in the
British Consul Library last week?"

"I have been there several times," I said. . . .

"You should try the American Library, too,"
he said, "I think it is very nice."

"You mean there is an American Library in
town?" I inquired. . . .

"Yes, the United States Information Service
Library," he answered. "As a matter of fact, that
is where I am going right now." . . .

I was no longer interested in going to the post
office. I was only interested in going to the library,
where I felt that the fact of its being operated and
run by the Americans would give me a sense of
being nearer to America. . . .

It was still February and a few days after I had
received the card confirming my membership at
the [American] library. I could check out books
now. There was one lying open on the table, left
there probably by the previous reader. I picked it
up, closed it, and looked at the title, *The Enduring*

Lincoln. I sat down and began reading. I came across the sentence, "The Whig Party was moribund." I rushed to the shelf to look for a dictionary to look up moribund.

Instead of the dictionary I saw the volume *American Junior Colleges.* I stopped all that I was doing or was going to do, and losing no time I picked up the volume. With rather shaky hands I opened it, not caring where the pages fell. They opened to "Skagit Valley Junior College, 1001 Lawrence, Mt. Vernon, Washington. Two year program, coeducational . . ." The volume went on to describe my future college. I copied the address. . . .

Skagit Valley College
Mount Vernon, Washington
February 29, 1960

Legson Kayira
P.O. Box 15075
Kibuye
Kampala, Uganda
B.E. Africa

Dear Mr. Kayira

We should be very happy to have you as a student here. We provide a scholarship for all foreign students. This covers all fees. We should be happy also to locate a job for you (if desired) which would take care of your board and room.

Please complete enclosed application for admission form and return to me. Keep me posted as to when

you would be coming. If there is any further information you desire, please let me know.

I am sending a copy of our current catalog under
separate cover (regular mail) for your information.

Yours sincerely
GEORGE HODSON
Dean

THE SUDAN

It was Sunday afternoon, September 25,
1960. . . .

"Yes, sir," she said as soon as she had put the
receiver back, "what can I do for you?"

"I am going to America," I breathed out. "I
want a visa."

"Do you have Form 1-20?"

"What?"

"Form 1-20."

I did not have it, indeed, I did not even know
what she was talking about. She began explaining
to me, saying that I could not be granted a visa
until I had this form, among other things. The
college should have sent me that form.

"I am sorry," she said. "I can only help you if
you get the form." . . .

A gentleman came into the office. . . .

"Your name is Legson Kayira?"

"Yes, sir."

"And you want a visa."

"Yes, sir."

"Where are you from, Mr. Kayira?"

"Nyasaland."

"And to which school are you going in the
United States?"

"Skagit Valley College, sir."

"Any correspondence with you from Skagit?"

"Yes, sir," I said. I unfolded two letters from my passport where I had kept them, and handed them to him. He read them through rather carefully and slowly.

"All right," he said. "How do you intend to get to America?"

"Walk to Port Said and work my way on a ship to New York," I said.

"Walk?" he said. "How did you get here from your home?"

"Walked most of the way," I said.

He took a paper and wrote something on it.

"When did you leave your home?"

"In 1958," I said.

"What time in 1958?"

"October." . . .

Mr. Coxson then handed me a piece of paper and a pencil, and asked me to write what I had told him. . . .

THE UNITED STATES

I did not know what to do. I was afraid, afraid of the thing that would take me to my destination. I was afraid the pilot would not see the airport since we were flying at night. We would be lost. Maybe he forgot to get some fuel. Maybe he forgot to check his engines. . . .

* * *

I was strolling down the long spacious corridors. I was alone. Suddenly a mysterious voice called, "Mr. Legson Kayira . . . calling Mr. Legson Kayira . . . please come to the counter." I stopped. I looked back and saw a few people way down the corridor, but they did not know me anymore than I knew them. There was nobody around me, but who was it that knew my name

already? I looked around again. I was still alone.
The few people down the corridor seemed uncon-
cerned about the mysterious voice. I took a deep
breath and shouted, "I am here . . . Legson
Kayira, I am here." Nobody heard me. The voice
stopped calling my name, and mystified as I was
by the whole thing, my heart thumped violently
in me. I turned and walked back to the BOAC
counter. I was at New York's Idlewild International Airport. . . .

It was late in the afternoon when we completed
the last hop of the trip. . . .

As soon as I stepped out I heard someone from
the ground shout, "Smile!" There were a number
of people standing there, some of them looking at
me through the fancy machines called cameras
which I was already getting used to. . . .

Mr. George Hodson, president of the College,
and Mr. Neil Hamburg, president of the Student
Body, were standing at the door, where a sign
was displayed reading simply, WELCOME LEG-
SON. . . .

The Christmas tree was glowing in its many
colors near a corner. Tables were neatly arranged.
. . . After dinner I addressed the party and in my
unprepared speech I expressed the hope that I
would do my best so that the great help they had
given me was not given in vain. . . .

I felt most tired now. The Atwoods then drove
me and the lady reporter to their home, my new
home, some ten miles or so northwest of the college.

I was stunned to discover that Santa Claus had
beaten me to the Atwoods, indeed, that he had
learned of me long before I knew him myself. I
found a long stocking bearing my name, hanging

on the wall, a package under the Christmas tree, and a bunch of letters. . . . On one of the walls hung a homemade calendar on which the Atwood children had been marking off the days up to the time of my arrival. . . .

Then it was Christmas. How different! How beautiful! I was used only to the simple and modest manner in which we celebrated it in my own village. No exciting preparations. Too far away for Santa Claus. No Christmas trees, no cards either. But early on Christmas morning little children ran about in the village shouting, "Christmas Box." Then families had their morning meals and cleaned themselves up. The believers, and nonbelievers if they wished, gathered together in a Church or a field. The pastor or maybe a local school teacher read the Testament, and then they gave thanks to their Maker for sacrificing His own Son to save them. The school children sang one or two carols, more often than not, "Silent Night." . . .

NYASALAND

Isn't it a beautiful coincidence that I should be writing this portion of the book under the roof of my mother's house? Oh no, I am not dreaming. I am really here. . . .

My mother is still here. . . . She is still young-looking and still unable to comprehend the fact that America is considerably more than five days away on foot but only about a day by jet. . . .

I can say that I feel like I am a child of two nations, appreciating two cultures, one that I was born to and the other that was once foreign to me, but which is now becoming familiar.

politics

For generations African societies have been active politically. Before Europeans came, Africans were highly involved in political decision-making. Sometimes the unit of power was as small as a group of families; sometimes it was as large as a highly centralized governmental hierarchy.

The colonial take-over by Europeans interrupted and superseded these power structures. Africans tried to participate in colonial government, but they were frequently mere puppets of controlling Europeans.

Educated Africans tried to compete with whites using European "rules of the game." For 100 years along the West African coast, a small group edited newspapers, wrote books, formed organizations: men like Bishop Crowther, Edward W. Blyden and Casely Hayford. Today they are heroes. The hero in Ekwensi's People of the City is named De Pereira, but in real life his name was probably Herbert Macaulay who led the Nigerian independence movement from 1908 til his death in 1946 at the age of 82. His political activity gave him the appellation, "the Father of Nigerian Nationalism."

Since 1960 several dozen new African nations have received their independence. Kachingwe tells about one nation's birth in No Easy Task. Here a Malawian man beyond moral question eases his people to independence and freedom—Uhuru. "The Old Man," as his journalist son calls him, forms a political organization whose efforts culminate in constitutional talks in London. The commissioned officer and the Municipal African Affairs Officer are both white men in this story. At the time of success his father treats his son equally as any other reporter. He also tells them he sees all of life, including the political, as religious. African leaders in real life who entered the political arena with deep religious conviction include Kenneth Kaunda, President of Zambia; Ndabaningi Sithole, now in prison in Rhodesia; and Chief Albert J. Luthuli, before his death the president of the African National Congress in the Union of South Africa.

In the struggle between East and West, Africa's own interests have been ignored. Around 1960, some African politicians believed their only hope of influencing world politics was to form a united states of Africa. They were also carried away by the euphoria of nationalism. Ekwensi shows in his novel, Beautiful Feathers, one honest man's attempt to bring this dream into full flower in the early 1960s. Wilson learns at an All Africa conference in Senegal that when the owner is not looking, the outsider will take his treasure away. In Ekwensi's allegory there is an animal hunt. Wilson, the naive, actually kills the animal; but the "American observer" runs off with the carcass *and trophy. The Americans get the prize because the Africans are fighting among themselves.*

The new political structure—the nation—is incomplete. The old political folkways and mores are not adequate for the new political scaffolding. The pressures of caring for the extended family and the possibilities of great personal power frequently lead to corruption.

Disillusionment with self-government among the ordinary people is well described by Ayi Kwei Armah in The Beautyful Ones Are Not Yet Born. *Perhaps there is some hope if the little men, the allocation clerks of Africa, doing their jobs well, may in the long run keep the country on the track. Armah writes about the days when Kwame Nkrumah was President of Ghana and corruption was commonplace. A military coup exiled Nkrumah in 1966. Exiled with it, Armah hopes, is the people's dependence on charismatic leaders to get them through.*

People of the City
Cyprian Ekwensi

By polling day all energy had been spent. The politicians were now tired of making promises and had taken their proper places—in the background. Clerks, motor drivers, butchers, market women, shopkeepers, who as responsible citizens had

From *People of the City,* © 1963 Cyprian Ekwensi (rev. ed.). Reprinted by permission of William Heinemann and Company, Ltd.

previously registered their names, went to the
polling stations that dotted the city, and cast their
votes. For that single day, the power was in their
hands and the politicians waited with beating
hearts and speculating eyes for the results.

It turned out that out of the fifty seats in the
Town Council the Self-Government Now Party
had won thirty-nine, leaving eleven seats for the
Realization Party. This meant that the government was now in the hands of the S.G.N. Party
and that they would elect a mayor from one of
their leaders.

There had never been a mayor in the West African city and now the first one was to be an African. It was a great triumph for the S.G.N. Party.
The *West African Sensation* had been working
hard on the elections with such leaders as:

WHO WILL BE MAYOR?
CHOICE OF MAYOR CAUSES SPLIT IN SELF-
   GOVERNMENT NOW PARTY
TIME TO REDEEM ELECTION PROMISES
REALIZATION PARTY THROWS BOMBSHELL
NATURAL RULERS AND THE NEW CONSTITU-
   TION

. . . There was a shortage of good men and it
was a loss to the paper to have a man of Amusa
Sango's calibre counting the minutes and doing
nothing.

Then the great opportunity came. It was on a
morning when the rain had added to his irritations
and he had come into the office soaked. He remembered stamping his shoes as he entered the
office. Layeni, the night editor, had not left. They
were all discussing a subject of national importance.

'A great shock for the nation . . . but anyway, he was an old man . . . Good-bye to the wizard of statesmanship, the inspiration for the new movement . . .'

'Without him, there would be no nationalism today on the West Coast . . .'

Sango knew they were talking about De Pereira, the greatest nationalist of all time. He was eighty-three and though he did not involve himself now in the physical campaigns and speech-makings he was the brains of the S.G.N. Party. For the last twenty years he had been the spiritual leader of the party and the party dramatized his ideals. . . .

And as he heard more and more he found what he had missed by not being an active nationalist. The city, the whole country, rose together to pay tribute to De Pereira. Almost within the hour the musicians were singing new songs in his name; merchants were selling cloth with imprints of his inspiriting head. Funeral editions of the *Sensation* featured his life story from the time of Queen Victoria of England to Queen Elizabeth II, in whose reign he died. They asked the question: in view of De Pereira's death at so critical a time in the history of the S.G.N. Party, who would guide them to ultimate victory for the whole nation? This was too much of a loss for African nationalism. Who else had the experience, the wizardry, the insight, the centuries-old diplomacy of this man who had so long defied death?

During the funeral not a single white man was to be seen in the streets of the city, or anywhere near the Cathedral Church of Christ where his body lay in state. Even those who lived near the Cathedral were shut off by those overflowing crowds that vied for one peep at the magnificent coffin. In the trees above and around the Cathedral people hung like monkeys. Some had even defied the captains of ships anchored in the lagoon and climbed on deck, bravely trespassing, unmoved by the heavy smoke pouring from the funnels.

Sango was seeing a new city—something with a feeling. The madness communicated itself to him, and in the heat of the moment he forgot his worldly inadequacies and threw himself with fervour into the spirit of the moment. . . . Two hundred thousand people forming themselves into an immovable block of fiery nationalists who jammed the streets, waiting, hoping to catch one glimpse of the coffin. Death had glorified De Pereira beyond all his dreams.

No Easy Task
Aubrey Kachingwe

There was already a huge multitude in the grounds of the Centre, and still more people were pouring in from all directions. I noticed a rather large number of policemen around. Their attitude was offensive, and most of them were impatient and bad-tempered. Perhaps because it was so hot. . . .

. . . I went to a commissioned officer. 'I am a

From *No Easy Task*, © Aubrey Kachingwe, 1966. Reprinted by permission of Heinemann Educational Books, Ltd.

Pressman,' I told him and fished out my card. 'I want to get into the Centre. I want to speak to the manager.'

'We have orders not to let anyone in. Not even the Governor,' he said.

'But I have got to see him.'

He examined me up and down. 'What is it you want him for?'

'I want to know what time the meeting is starting, and I want to take my things from there.'

'All right. Go in, but don't be long.'

I did not even thank him.

Ben was in his office, sitting behind his desk, doing nothing, sulking. 'The meeting should have started already by now—what's happening, Ben?' . . . .

'There is no meeting. . . . The authorities refused to issue a permit for the meeting. They claim the notice was too short. . . .

We got out and saw a crowd pushing towards a police van with a number of people jammed in the back. Worried policemen were pushing the noisy crowd back from the vehicle, now slowly moving away. The crowd closed around it, and the situation seemed critical. . . .

The District Commissioner for Urban Area drove up with two high-ranking police officers and a heavy escort. . . . He was a tall man wearing a short-sleeved khaki shirt and khaki shorts; he stood erect, his white, clean-shaven face betraying no emotion. . . .

'This is an illegal gathering. No permit was issued for any meeting here today. Now, I want everyone here to disperse peacefully. Each and every one of you, go home.' . . . Nobody moved. . . . Then he fished out a piece of paper from one of his pockets.

'This is the Riot Act and I am reading it.' . . .
The Riot Squad was on the ready, and only
waited for his one word to strike.

Just as the situation was getting out of control,
a lone voice was heard above the murmur: 'My
people. Listen to me.' The voice came from behind the crowd. I looked up, and saw an old man
hoisted up above everybody else. *My father!* My
God, what was he doing?

'Go home, my people. Disperse. We do not
want trouble. Don't let yourselves be mowed
down because of acting against the authorities.
We are a peaceful people, and God-fearing. Let
your leaders fight for you. We will claim our rights
the correct way. I appeal to each of you to go
home. We shall call for a meeting soon. Go, my
people. Children of God.'

Miraculously, the crowd started to melt.

'Our good Josiah . . .' they chanted.

'Long live brave old Josiah. . . .'

He was carried from shoulder to shoulder up to
his car. . . . But hardly had they closed the door
when a policeman leaned in and dragged them
out. In a moment he was joined by several other
policemen, and given cover by the Riot Squad,
they shoved the old man and the two boys into a
police vehicle and hurried them away.

At this the crowd was enraged. . . . Why had
the police provoked the crowd by removing the
old man? . . .

By now things were really hot. . . . The police in turn made baton charges, threw tear-gas
bombs, and filled all the trucks available with
screaming men and women. . . .

Night came. . . . Felix and father were still
held. . . .

'We better wait here,' Mary said. 'Father is an

old man—they will probably let him come home
for the night.'

Although she said this, we knew they would not
free him so soon. . . .

* * *

It was a beautiful day, early in the spring. A
very big crowd assembled at the stadium—the
biggest perhaps that had ever assembled there so
far. . . . My father took the chair in the centre
of the front row. . . .

The Old Man harangued the crowd for three
hours, and you could feel the atmosphere working
up to a feverish pitch as he went on mentioning
one thing after another. . . . 'Something must be
done, now. And I mean just that. Now, now,
now.' . . .

The Old Man's performance astounded me, and
I was seeing a new man, almost a different man
from the man I had always known as my humble
parson father. . . .

* * *

Mass meetings were held at different places
throughout the country in the weeks that followed.
The Organization, now known as *Banja*—the
Family—spread like wild fire, swept the towns
and the countryside. The Old Man became a
household name; even little children knew the
name. . . .

* * *

Bill Akimu and I were sitting in the general office. . . .

For a while we typed in silence—the machines
making a monotonous tapping sound.

Then Bill looked up from his work. 'Jo, . . .

This is the beginning of great things for our country.'

I looked at my watch. . . .

'Where do you think they are now?' I asked. . . .

'I should say they are flying over Sudan or Egypt, now. They left by the 2 P.M. plane this afternoon, presumably,' he said. . . . 'They will be having breakfast in London barely a day after leaving home. The world is indeed small now!'

'When does the Governor go?' I asked.

'Day after tomorrow,' Bill said. 'And the *Akapilikoni* leave tomorrow.'

'This is a very unexpected thing,' I said. 'It will take everyone in the country by surprise. . . .

'. . . There is nothing the Government could do but relent—let the people out, and talk with them. That is why they are all going to England to talk over the next stage of the country's progress with the leaders of the people taking a full part, unlike in the past.' . . .

So it was true the Old Man and three of his colleagues had been flown to London for Constitutional talks to start in a few days time with the British Government. . . .

. . . Everywhere in the Location there was noise of joy—tins being whacked, drums sounded, women shrilling—all very exciting.

[Al said,] 'This is great, Jo. . . . Living at a time when history is being made. . . . Right now, man, we the owners of the country are moulding the destiny of our country—shaping the future of our children, and of their children —of posterity.'

* * *

The airport was six miles from Kawacha Town.

. . . The crowd outside the tall terminal building, now numbering over 50,000 yelled into a
thunderous noise, drowning even the sound of the
aircraft's engines.

Then the Old Man came out. . . .

'Kwaaacha,' he shouted. *'Uhuru!'* . . . .

He, like the younger men, was wearing a well-
cut London suit of a light, dark material. I thought
he looked younger and handsomer. . . .

As he spoke, I noticed that he had fitted himself
with a complete set of teeth which looked almost
natural. His cheeks were now rounder than before. He spoke with confidence and was master of
the situation. My father had changed very much,
I thought. Several times I tried to attract his attention to me; as his son, he should have shown more
interest in me. After all, we had not seen each
other for many months. That was what I thought,
but my father gave me no preferential treatment
over the other journalists. I could well be no relative of his, for all it seemed there.

He is not just my father. He is a father of all of
us—of the country.

'The talks in London concerning the constitutional changes of this country went on very well
indeed. My colleagues and I have been able to
make the case of our people here, in this country,
not only heeded, but accepted in a big measure,'
the Old Man said. 'In a few words, I will tell you,
gentlemen, that the results have been even better
than we expected. . . .

'Now, we hope that my Organization will be
able to sweep the elections. . . . We mean to
rule ourselves.' . . .

Somebody asked, 'Will you quit being a minister of the Church, sir?'

'How can that be, my friend?' The Old Man retorted. 'What you seem to suggest is that I shall cease to serve God's children because I am a politician. That is really a wrong way of looking at it. As a minister, I serve God through the Church,' the Old Man said. 'You, myself and all the people in this country and elsewhere, are all the children of God. If you helped me in my troubles—say I was sick—you are serving God. But if you let me suffer when you could easily render help, you are not fully serving God even if you were a minister, a sheikh or a patriarch.

'My African people in this country suffer many disadvantages,' he said. 'They do not enjoy many of the things that God has given us, and yet, these things are there and being denied them, although other people enjoy them. . . . Besides serving God in the Church, I also will serve Him by helping my people in their struggle to regain the right to enjoy with the others what God gave them to enjoy.'

Beautiful Feathers
Cyprian Ekwensi

All through the plane journey he lay on his back in a kind of stupor. It was a special plane and he had memories of the elegant air hostess who kept changing her frock at every stop—there

From *Beautiful Feathers,* © Cyprian Ekwensi, 1963. Reprinted by permission of Hutchinson Publishing Group, Ltd. and David Higham Associates, London.

must have been ten stops at least—between Lagos and Dakar. . . .

He tried not to think of the conference. . . . Men drifted about the plane, black men in light-weight suits who spoke French, American, English, Somali, Yoruba, Hausa. Wilson tried to classify them. Those who spoke French he immediately classified as coming from the ex-French territories. The American-accented ones must come from Liberia, and the African language and English ones from other parts of Africa. . . .

As soon as he descended, the group came towards him. . . .

'Welcome . . . have you had a good flight? Welcome.'

Wilson looked about him and immediately the burning hope of Africa was here evident. These men were all black and they carried brief-cases and looked as if the future of the world was tucked away under their armpits. Brotherly love glowed on their faces, and patriotism, loyalty and, above all . . . fight. African Solidarity. African Unity. Wilson heard the phrase over and over. African Solidarity. Something in their attitude spoke to him.

It seemed to say: *We are here to live, to find ways, to seek for truth. No blind decisions. We are here, like the morning light, to shine our mark on everything.* . . .

Wilson walked towards the Independence Square in Dakar, his brief-case tucked under his arm. . . .

At the entrance to the Ministry he stopped to admire the guards in their musketeers' red cloaks, scarlet drapings and shiny black skins. They reminded him of some weird dream, and when the black men in the jet-black Citroens began to arrive he was afraid. This was a strange process in reverse, and yet the Africans were taking it all normally.

And then the Nigerian Minister of Conferences was there and they were talking tactics. A guard broke into the discussions and told them they were awaited. The Minister of Conferences spoke a little more and they all rose and walked along the marble floor towards the conference room. . . .

* * *

At the week-end the hunting party set out for the game fields outside Dakar. Wilson led the Nigerian team and from other parts of Africa very important people formed the team. Americans, Russians, British and French observers brought up the rear—as gun-bearers. Wilson saw now that things were working in reverse. The black man could hold his head high: one of the many joys of Independence, reversing the course of history.

The white men did not complain, but were silent, and no one suspected anything. Occasionally they met and whispered among themselves or laughed. Wilson called aside a delegate and tried to tell him: 'Look, the world is watching and listening. We must behave our best!'

'Non compres pas!'

The delegate shrugged his shoulders and walked off into the woods, and at that moment a huge beast shaped like a rhino, but infinitely more elegant, came charging down towards them. Wilson fired, but he also heard the sound of other shots, three or four—before the beast stumbled, leaving a trail of blood, shattered shrubs and indistinct footprints which they followed till they came to the riverside.

Wilson was among the first to reach the dead

beast. It was a very rare specimen and no one
could name it, but everyone believed it was highly
prized. Some of the hunters wanted the horns,
some wanted the whole beast preserved in a mu-
seum, and immediately an argument arose and
voices become loud. Nobody knew who squeezed
a trigger. There was the sharp crack of a shot and
everyone ran for cover. Confusion spread.

Wilson saw the white men carrying off the beast
and running down the slope. He aimed at the retreating white men, but a shot struck him in the
ribs and he fell. He lay there in a shot-riddled
mist, choking for breath, while his body floated in
endless circles, weightless.

* * *

Wilson opened his eyes and saw standing by his
bed a female nurse, attentive, listening. He identified the seated man as the President. . . .

'I have heard what happened when you went
shooting in the bush. It was for sport, yes?'

'For sport, Excellency!'

The President shook his head sadly. 'You know
. . . it is like the struggle for African Unity.
While Africa burns, interested parties carry away
the loot. We must be on our guard, must be ready
to give and take. . . . This for your efforts,
M'sieur Iyari.' He pinned the glittering object [in-
signia of honor] on Wilson's shirt and shook him
by the hand. Wilson saluted as best he
could. . . .

* * *

To Wilson it seemed as if his Prime Minister
had not moved one inch since he saw him last. He
had been away for two months, not ten days, as
planned, and now he was back in Lagos and the

Prime Minister was lying back on the couch, re-laxed and smiling. . . .

'My dear Mr. Iyari. You are a young man.' His voice fell one octave. 'A very young man, and therefore impatient. You lead a strike here be-cause you thought Nigeria was this, Nigeria was that. Now you've seen for yourself how a very lit-tle thing can upset unity. But we must keep try-ing.'

'It was surprising, sir. I couldn't understand it.'

'It's human nature. I mean, you all began shoot-ing at one another. Friends! Did you go there to shoot at one another or to shake hands?'

Wilson was silent.

The Beautyful Ones Are
Not Yet Born
Ayi Kwei Armah

The dimness of the morning made all colors in-side the office itself look very strange. . . . At the control desk the night clerk was still in his seat but he had fallen asleep. . . . The man walked noiselessly toward the sleeper and touched him very gently. . . .

"What? What?" the clerk asked, his voice un-easy, almost shouting.

The man looked levelly at the waking sleeper and smiled. The smile seemed to reassure the clerk, and the terror vanished from his face.

"Ah, contrey," he said. "I tire. . . .

From *The Beautyful Ones Are Not Yet Born*, by Ayi Kwei Armah. Reprinted by permission of Houghton Mifflin Company.

"There was a lot of work last night?" the man asked.

"No, contrey," said the other, "not work. But when man is alone all through the night . . ."

"I know," said the man, also shaking his head.

"Oh you don't know, contrey," the clerk continued, as if he had not heard. "You don't know how last night was bad for me."

"What happened?"

For a long time the clerk gave no answer, only staring at the man as if something about him aroused a huge amount of suspicion. Then with a suddenness that amazed the listening man, he said, "Nothing. Nothing, contrey, nothing. But I sat here alone, and I was wishing somebody would come in, and all night long there was nobody. Me alone."

"Anyway . . . nothing went wrong?"

"No," the clerk said. "At Kojokrom the control telephone is dead again."

"As usual.". . .

The man looked at the control graph above the big desk. The lines were not too many, and only two of them were red. Passenger trains. . . .

After eight the office began filling up rapidly as the day clerks came in with their little jokes and the talk of brief pay days and perennial Passion Weeks. . . .

After twelve even those within could tell the sun had risen very high. . . . Everybody seemed to sweat a lot, not from the exertion of their jobs, but from some kind of inner struggle that was always going on. So the sea salt and the sweat together and the fan above made this stewy atmosphere in which the suffering sleepers came and worked and went dumbly back afterward to homes they had earlier fled. There was really no doubt that it was like that in all their homes, everywhere save for those who had found in themselves the hardness for the upward climb. And *he* was not one of those. . . .

At a time like this, when the month was so far gone and all there was was the half-life of Passion Week, lunchtime was not a time to refresh oneself. Unless, of course, one chose to join the increasing numbers who had decided they were so deep in despair that there was nothing worse to fear in life. These were the men who had finally, and so early, so surprisingly early, seen enough of something in their own lives and in the lives of those around them to convince them of the final futility of efforts to break the mean monthly cycle of debt and borrowing, borrowing and debt. Nothing was left beyond the necessity of digging oneself deeper and deeper into holes in which there could never be anything like life. . . .

In through the door came a belly swathed in *kente* cloth. . . .

"Good even," the visitor shouted, moving forward.

"Evening.". . .

"I am looking for the allocations clerk," the visitor said.

"Which one? . . . There are two clerks. One for time, one for wagon space."

"Aha, I understand now. . . . Wagons. It's wagons I have come to talk about."

"Space allocation. You should come earlier in the day, though. In this office also the clerks go home at four-thirty."

"Oh, I know," the teeth said, "I know, but I thought he would stay after work."

"Had you a fixed time with him?"

"Actually, no. But someone told me this was about the right time to come."

"To come for what?" the man asked.

". . . actually, it is a bit private.". . .

Then he seemed to make up his mind about the thing that was making him so restless.

"Brother," the many teeth said, "brother, you also can help me."

"Me?" The man had not expected this.

"Yes, brother . . . And I will make you know that you have really helped me.". . .

"I am not the booking clerk," the man said. "The booking clerk has gone hime.". . .

"My friend," he said, "all joke aside. . . . Why do you have to treat me like that? What do you want?"

"I am sorry," the man answered, "but I have nothing to do with allocations. . . . I have my job; the booking clerk has his job. I don't interfere with him.". . .

"You can see that clerk for me." The visitor looked suspiciously toward the door, then plunged his left arm underneath his *kente* folds. When the arm emerged it was clutching a dark brown leather wallet. The wallet was not fat. The man looked steadily at the visitor. The visitor's gaze was bent, his eyes looking in the wallet while thick fingers fumbled inside. Then the fingers brought out two carefully held-out notes, two green tens. The man said nothing. . . .

"Take it," the visitor said. "One for you, one for him."

"Why should I?". . .

"You are a funny man, you this man," he said. "You think I am a fool to be giving you just ten cedis? . . . Is nothing. I know ten is nothing. So, my friend, what do you drink?"

The man looked levelly at the visitor and gave his answer. "Water.". . .

"I beg you, let us stop joking now. . . . They are waiting for me and I must go. A man is a man. I tell you what I will do. Take that one for yourself and give the other one to your friend. I myself will find some fine drink for you. Take it. Take it, my friend."

The man looked at the face before him, pleading with the words of millions and the voices of ages, and he felt lonely in the way only a man condemned by all things around him can ever feel lonely. "I will not take it," he said, too quietly, perhaps.

The visitor did not touch his money. He did not even look at it. He only said, "Look, I mean it. I offer you three times. Is good money."

"I know."

"Then take it."

"No.". . .

"You refuse?"

"Yes.". . .

"But why? . . . why do you treat me so? What have I done against you? Tell me, what have I done? . . . Why do you behave like that? . . . Tomorrow, what will you say to the other man?"

"Nothing."

* * *

Silence. No voices, no sounds in the night, just silence. The man walked into the hall, meeting the eyes of his waiting wife. These eyes are flat, the

eyes of a person who has come to a decision not
to say anything; eyes totally accepting and un-
questioning in the way only a thing from which
nothing is ever expected can be accepted and not
questioned. . . .

The children begin to come out of the room
within. They are not asleep, not even the third
little one. It seems their eyes also are learning this
flat look that is a defense against hope. . . . The
man moves forward and sits at [the table] with
his back to his guilt, resolving to break the heavy
quiet.

"I saw Koomson on my way home," he
says.

"And Estella was with him, I suppose?" she
asks at last.

"Uh-huh.". . .

"Mmmmmmmmmm. . . . She has married well.
. . . Life has treated her well."

"Koomson says he wants to come and see us.
Sunday, nine."

"Mmmmmmm."

"That probably means your mother, not us. We
should remember to tell her when she comes."

. . . "It is not only for my mother that Koomson will come."

"What do you mean?". . .

"I mean if things go well, they will go well for
all of us."

"Do you think so?". . .

"Why are you trying to cut yourself apart from
what goes for all of us?"

"I did not know," the man says very slowly, "I
did not know that I had agreed to join anything.
. . . Where is Koomson getting all the money for
this boat?". . .

"He is getting it." Flat finality.

"All right," says the man. "Let us say I am not in it.". . .

The man looks at his wife and finds her eyes fixed on his face. "What were you saying?" he asks.

"Nothing," she says . . .

"Somebody offered me a bribe today," he says after a while.

"Mmmmmmm!"

"One of those timber contractors."

"Mmmmmmm. To do what?"

"To get him an allocation."

"And like an Onward Christian Soldier you refused?"

The sudden vehemence of the question takes the man completely by surprise. "Like a what?"

* * *

"On-ward Chris-tian Soooooooldier!
Maaarching as to Waaaaaaaaar
With the Cross of Jeeeeeeesus
Goooing on be-fooooooore!"

The man took a long look at his wife's face. Then he said, "It wasn't even necessary."

"What were you afraid of then?" the woman asked.

"But why should I take it?"

"And why not? . . . Maybe you like this crawling that we do, but I am tired of it. I would like to have someone drive me where I want to go."

"Like Estella Koomson?"

"Yes, like Estella. And why not? Is she more than I?"

"We don't know how she got what she has," the man said.

"And we don't care. . . . We don't care. Why pretend? Everybody is swimming toward what he wants.". . .

"Is that the way you see things now?" he asked her.

"Have you found some other way?"

"No.". . .

There was nothing the man could say to his wife, and the woman herself did not look as if she thought there could be anything said to her about what she knew was so true. But inside the man the confusion and the impotence had swollen into something asking for a way out of confinement, and in his restlessness he rose and went out very quietly through the door, and his wife sat there not even staring after him, not even asking him where he was going or when he would come back in the night, or even whether he wanted to return at all to this home. . . .

* * *

How horribly rapid everything has been, from the days when men were not ashamed to talk of souls and of suffering and of hope, to these low days of smiles that will never again be sly enough to hide the knowledge of betrayal and deceit. There is something of an irresistible horror in such quick decay. . . .

* * *

It is not true at all that when men are desperate they will raise their arms and welcome just anybody who comes talking of their salvation. . . .

How long will Africa be cursed with its leaders?
There were men dying from the loss of hope, and
others were finding gaudy ways to enjoy power
they did not have. We were ready here for big and
beautiful things, but what we had was our own
black men hugging new paunches scrambling to
ask the white man to welcome them onto our
backs. These men who were to lead us out of our
despair, they came like men already grown fat and
cynical with the eating of centuries of power they
had never struggled for, old before they had even
been born into power, and ready only for the
grave. . . .

There is something so terrible in watching a
black man trying at all points to be the dark ghost
of a European, and that was what we were seeing
in those days. . . . We knew then, and we know
now, that the only real power a black man can
have will come from black people. . . .

* * *

When he opens the office door there is loud,
pleased laughter inside, and a voice with a vague
familiarity says, "No. This is only your *kola*. Take
it as *kola*." Another laugh. "I was sure you would
understand, if only I could find you properly. My
friend, if you get the logs moving for me, I will see
you again. Don't worry. I will take you to my own
house."

"It's all right," the allocations clerk kept saying.
"It's all right.". . .

The allocations clerk is in there with his boss
for something like half an hour, and when he
emerges he is closely followed by the supervisor
and they are both smiling broad, very satisfied

smiles. Let them smile. This place is kind to them,
so let them smile. In another country they would
be in jail. Here they are heroes.

* * *

In the early morning the man let the world
around him lose itself softly in the growing pattern
of the railway graph above the desk in front of
him. Sometimes he could forget himself and almost everything else, concerning himself with the
job alone, doing everything that was necessary.
. . . At least the job itself was one of the few
around which did not have a killing dullness.
There really was a definite kind of beauty to the
growth of the daily maze on the graph sheet, and
a satisfaction in seeing the penciled lines crossing
the time and station lines, red lines for passenger
trains, lead pencil lines for goods trains, blue for
manganese. . . .

It was not until after eight o'clock that the
other staff started coming in. When, at half past
seven, not even the messengers had come, the
man had wondered what could have happened,
but in a while he took his mind off the matter. The
messengers were, as usual, the first to arrive. One
of them came in like a ghost, so quietly in fact that
the man did not notice him till the other arrived.
This one came whistling. . . . But the other messenger shut his companion up. The second could
not bear the silence long, and, walking around behind the man, he sighed very loudly and exclaimed, "Ei, these *coups!*"

The man did not turn around, but he asked the
messenger, "Has there been another one?"

"Yes, man!"

"In Africa or somewhere else?"

"Today, today, here in Ghana!"

Now the other messenger walked out of his corner and joined the two. "So you haven't heard?"

"On the morning shift we can't hear the news," the man said.

"No six o'clock news this morning. Only some strange announcement by a man with a strange name, then *soja* music. They say they have seized power."

"Who?" the man asked.

"Army men and policemen."

"Oh, I see. I thought they always had power. Together with Nkrumah and his fat men."

The messengers said nothing. Even the one who had come in whistling had a sort of second fear in his eyes, the kind of look people have when they are unsure of what they are doing, and want to take care to be able to claim that it was all a joke, should the need arise. In the man's own mind there was a diffuse uncertainty. What, after all, could it mean? One man, with the help of people who loved him and believed in him, had arrived at power and used it for himself. Now other men, with the help of guns, had come to this same power. What would it mean?

The senior men did not come to work. Fear was a very strong thing in their lives, and it was understandable that they would want to wait when something like this was happening. . . .

The other junior staff came one by one, adding little bits, some very wild indeed, to the news available. . . .

When the sun had gone up there was the sound of some commotion in the street outside. A man who had been a trade unionist for the overthrown government rushed into the office announcing the *coup* as if he had himself accomplished it. Then he ordered people to go out and show their loyalty to the new men of power. With a silence that spoke everybody's shame, the men in the office went out singly to join the crowd outside. . . .

The man did not move from his desk. The old-new union man stood staring at him, then said, "Contrey, what about you?"

"Yes, what about what?"

"We are all demonstrating."

"For what?"

"Don't you know there is a new government?"

"They tell me so. But I know nothing about the men. What will I be demonstrating for?"

"Look, contrey, if you don't want trouble, get out."

"If two trains collide while I'm demonstrating, will you take the responsibility?"

"Oh," said the organizer, "if it is the job, fine. But we won't tolerate any Nkrumaists now."

"You know," said the man slowly, "you know who the real Nkrumaists are.". . .

The evening shift man came only a few minutes late. . . . The streets were very quiet. . . . As he turned along the road to go home, the man felt completely apart from all that was taking place. He would like to know about it, but there would be plenty of time for it, and he was not burdened with any hopes that new things, really new things, were as yet ready to come out. Someday in the long future a new life would maybe flower in the country, but when it came, it would not choose as its instruments the same people who had made a habit of killing new flowers. The future goodness may come eventually, but before then where were the things in the present which would prepare the way for it?

economics

The black people in Africa are poor. Most earn less than $100 per year. One group of poor Africans are the farmers who cannot hope to harvest more than their arms and backs can produce. Farming is organized around the extended family system. These people have food to eat, but they have little for anything else. In Kinsman and Foreman, *Aluko describes an isolated district in Western Nigeria in the 1950s at the end of the colonial period. What the British officer calls "graft" is considered by the local inhabitants to be "charity at home." The local church supports the prevailing mores; part of the money gained from a parishioner's graft helps support the church. The local son, who "made good" as an engineer and is appointed to manage his home district, has adopted Western attitudes and is in continuous conflict with his family.

Another group of poverty-stricken black Africans reside where farming has been mechanized and the land has been confiscated by a white rul-

*ing class. White settlers still own many of the
largest and most productive farms in independent
Africa: rubber in Liberia; coffee in French-speak-
ing areas; sisal, tea, coffee, tobacco and sugar. In
southern Africa whites own all the best farming
lands. East, central and southern African societies
are divided sharply into different occupational
classes: rich white land owners, medium income
Asian distributors, poor black laborers. Ngugi, in*
Weep Not, Child, *penetrates the grief which one
Kikuyu family suffers at the loss of its land to
white settlers. Ngotho, the father, tells the crea-
tion myth of the Kikuyu people, much like the
Adam and Eve story in the Book of Genesis, with
its detail of the first man and the first woman,
darkness and light, and "a holy tree." The story
moves swiftly to the single most important political question for the Kikuyu people: "Where did
the land go?" Then the oldest living son asks his
father, who is now an impotent black squatter, the
most important moral question: "How can you
continue working for a man who has taken your
land?"*

*Still another kind of poverty in Africa exists in
the urban slums surrounding mines, factories and
harbors. In* Mine Boy, *Peter Abrahams describes
the slums of Johannesburg. Most of the miners are
forced to live in all-male compounds for months
at a time. They are not permitted to leave. They
put up with this lack of freedom in order to earn
a few dollars to take back, eventually, to their
families in rural villages. Often they must pay
taxes on these meager earnings to white governments. Xuma has come to the city voluntarily. His
white boss turns out to be a generous-hearted
Irishman named Paddy who immediately likes*

Xuma and encourages his natural leadership with the miners underground.

In this story one sees institutional racism at work. Paddy arranges to give eight pounds in South African currency from his own pocket to an African dying of mine disease and procures for him a train ticket so he can return to his home village. But Paddy cannot arrange to change the mining system that enslaves thousands of miners and exploits them for its own tremendous profit. Paddy is not a racist; but the mining company is a racist institution. In 1970 a white miner in South Africa earns $420 a month. The black miner, who is known to the company not by name but by an identity number, makes $28 a month. And they do about the same work. But white workers make 20 times as much as black ones. In similar proportions the West devours the wealth of the whole world. Americans, only 6 percent of the world's population, use up (according to Erik Severeid) 40 percent of the world's resources each year.

Urban and rural change are closely intertwined. In *The Gab Boys,* Cameron Duodu tells about a little Ghanaian village, Pusupusu. Dozens of teen-aged boys have finished ten years of schooling and have no hopes of continuing. They reject their fathers' subsistence farming career. There are no other jobs in the village. About to be fined in court as nuisances, they run away. Asamoah gets a job with the Tema Railway because of special assistance from the Anglican rector's daughter. "Luck, luck had been my lot. Why me and not them?" Asamoah asks himself. Asamoah asks in his loneliness, Shouldn't a village feel some responsibility toward those who have been raised in it? Only when one of the Gab Boys is killed do they come *home for the funeral and discover the village does call them sons.*

In 1960 W. W. Rostow wrote very simply about the stages of economic development. He suggested that the U.S.A., Canada and Europe were in stage V (High Mass-Consumption), that the Soviet Union and Japan were in stage IV (Maturity), that Mexico, Argentina, Turkey and others were in stage III (Take-Off). In 1960, then, he held that all the independent African nations were no further than stage II (obtaining the Preconditions for Take-Off). Some had not yet moved away from stage I (Traditional Economy). Stage II was described as a position in which economic progress was considered possible and good, and education necessary. In this condition people also believed new types of entrepreneurs should be encouraged, banks should be founded, and transportation and communications networks should be built.

It is at stage II that a young graduate engineer, Sekoni, in The Interpreters *by Soyinka, comes home to Nigeria from England. He is a Northern Nigerian and a Muslim. He has loved a Christian girl and his father has cursed him for it. Sekoni has a big dream. His dream is to build for the future Take-Off period of economic growth: to make electricity for little villages.*

But he is too dedicated. So, first, the Civil Service tries to turn him into an air-conditioned bureaucrat—this man who wants to "channel earth and sprout derricks." Next, they farm him out to a "bush" village to build a generator. Finally, they bribe a white specialist (an "expatriate expert") to report that Sekoni's generator will not work; whereupon the Civil Servants write off the project

*as a "loss" and add a huge profit to their personal
bankroll. Such squandering of resources postpones
still longer the time when the new nations can
enter the "Take-Off." And poverty continues.*

Kinsman and Foreman
T. M. Aluko

As soon as he entered the long parlour a spon-
taneous outburst of wailing greeted Titus from the
other end. . . .

He knew it was the custom. He knew that
whenever any member of the family arrives back
from a distant place, the clan gathers together and
wails together over the loss of this or that dear one
who had died whilst the new arrival was ab-
sent. . . .

'Enough! It is enough!' the man on the chair
next to him cried in a voice of authority. He at
once recognized the voice to be that of his great-
uncle Joel. . . .

'We are all here, both sides of the family. I want
you all to listen patiently to the words of my
mouth. I am an old man, and I must not speak too
long. . . . This child that has come back to us
from the country of the white man is going to hold
the post of a white man in Government work.
There is no other African who knows the work as
well as he does. That is why he is going to be given

From *Kinsman and Foreman*, © T. M. Aluko, 1966. Reprinted by permission of Heinemann Educational Books,
Ltd.

the post of a white man. It is a very delicate and
dangerous thing for a young man to be holding
such a very high post. We must see to it that he is
properly armed. And this is the reason why I am
here this morning, to hand my child Titus to his
kinsman Simeon.' . . .

'And you, Titus, you must listen to the words
of my mouth. Where Simeon tells you to go, you
must go. Where he tells you there is no way, know
there is no way; turn back. Associate with the men
he tells you are safe. Avoid those he points out to
you as dangerous. Let the eyes of Simeon be your
eyes from this day on; let his hands be your
hands. . . .

'Amen. It must be so. For I speak these words
at dawn.' . . . One of the women entered one of
the four rooms opening out into the parlour. She
brought out an enamel dish which she held before
the old man kneeling. Old Joel selected a big kola
nut from inside it.

'This is a kola nut. . . . With this kola nut I
invoke the spirit of Oluode to come to our midst.
I know that you, Oluode, our great ancestor, are
now with us. I can see you, because I am an old
man and I shall soon qualify to come to you; these
others cannot see you because they are still young.
Those of them that are not young are women, that
is why they cannot see you. I call you to be witness of the vow that these two descendants of
yours make at this solemn hour, before cock-
crow.' . . .

'A brother that shares kola with a brother and
engages in an act that can lead his brother to
trouble commits treachery. He incurs the displeas-
ure of Oluode. Oluode never forgives treachery.' . . .

* * *

Richard McBain, Provincial Engineer of the Department of Public Works, Ibadan, had been most disappointed at the official letter from headquarters informing him that a new arrival, a Nigerian by the name of Oti, had been posted to his Province to take over Ibala District. . . .

'So headquarters has sent you to take over Ibala District, Mr. Oti? . . . I had asked for someone experienced in both labour control and in financial control. I see this is your first tour, Mr. Oti? . . . I am afraid you will not find things here as easy as your college professors made you believe they were, back home in the University. You will find them not exactly answering to the methods you learnt in Differential Calculus and Theory of Structures and Fluid Mechanics—all the stuff in the books. Here you will be dealing with men, money and materials. And here in Nigeria you will find that all three behave most strangely.' . . .

. . . 'Just one thing, Mr. McBain. I rather gather that I'm being posted to be District Engineer, Ibala.' . . .

'Ibala is my home-town. . . . This is a matter about which I feel very strongly. My people would make my work nearly impossible. They would descend upon me in large numbers at all hours of the day. They'd want this—they'd want that. . . . Can't you change the posting?'

'Impossible. . . .'

* * *

The morning service at All Souls Church, Ibala, the following Sunday, was a special one for the family of Sister Deborah. . . .

The Rev. Michael Morakinyo read out the first of his two texts from the Book of Revelation, Chapter 14, verse 13. . . . The preacher read out his second text from the ninth chapter of the Book of Proverbs, verse 10. . . .

After the singing of the post-sermon hymn the pastor announced that the wives and children, the relatives and well-wishers of the late Elder Samuel Oti should come forward in a body to the altar for blessing. They all trooped out, led by the old man Joel, and followed by Sister Deborah, Titus and all the rest. . . . The crowd had hardly resumed their seats when the pastor made another announcement. The family and friends and well-wishers of Engineer Titus Oti, B. Sc. (Eng.) (London) would now come forward to the altar for thanksgiving and blessing. . . .

* * *

Titus was cross with his mother and he told her so. 'How many times will I tell you that if you want to come and see me you should send someone to tell me. I'll come to fetch you in my car. Do you have to walk from one end of the town to the other to get to me here at the Government Reservation? And now you are soaking wet.'

His mother in her turn was cross with him. 'Whenever I come to you you scold me as if I'm a little child of yesterday. I'm not. If it was not important for me to come I would not have come. And do I complain to you that I'm tired of walking? It's my feet and not yours that I use—why do you have to complain?' . . .

'And tell me now what the important matter is that has brought you here.'

'This letter,' she said. She untied the knot at one corner of her head-tie. She brought out a crumpled envelope which she handed to him. . . .

'Pastor and Foreman told me it is very important,' she said as he began to read the note. 'So I decided to bring it myself.' . . .

She noticed the frown on his face. 'What has Pastor written in the letter, Titus?'

'He and his Harvest Committee want me to open the Bazaar Sales.'

'They want you to open the Bazaar Sales!' she echoed. 'That is going to be serious. I don't want you to be exposed to the glare of the public yet, Titus.'

Titus shared her anxiety. For once mother and son appeared to agree.

'When women who are older than I see you performing this very important function they will be jealous, because their own sons are not as important as my son. That is why I am anxious. I am afraid of witches and evil-doers. . . . But we must accept the invitation since it has something to do with the church. . . . If we don't, they will think we are running away from spending money. We must begin to prepare for it now.'

'What do we prepare—and how many of us?' he asked. . . .

'Can you do it for less than £30? When your kinsman, the Foreman, did it last year he opened it with more than that. He spent about £40.'

'More than £30! Where did he get the money from?' . . .

'He is quite rich, Titus. And you too will soon be rich. You both do the same work and people who do this work have plenty of money. Everyone says so. And I know it's true.'

'But, Mother, I don't want you to talk like this,' he stopped her. 'I have no money, and I'm going to be honest. I'm not going to steal any money, to please anyone. If the Church people want £30 from me for opening Bazaar Sales, they will be disappointed. I just haven't got it.'

'But, Titus, you mustn't talk like that. You mustn't let down the family. We shall find the money.' . . .

'I'll drive you back home. How's my great-aunt today?'

'She is well. But people of her age die without warning—without being ill. So you must begin to put money aside now for the funeral expenses.'

'Money for Bazaar Sales! Money for funeral expenses! Money for this, money for that. Christ in heaven! It's nothing but money, money, and yet more money ever since I came back from England!'

'Titus!'

On the drive back to his mother's home Titus pondered the problem of money and allied matters. Before he left England he had been told at the Colonial Office that his salary on arrival in Nigeria would be forty-two pounds ten shillings a month. He and Bola had thought that that was a reasonably good salary and that he should be able to save at least twelve pounds ten shillings out of this every month. Surely one pound a day was sufficient to live on.

He had been back from England five months now. And in every one of these five months there had been demands on his purse. One pound a day had not been sufficient to live on at all.

* * *

Pa Joel did not succeed in his determination to knock sense into the head of Titus. There were

angry scenes between the old man and the young
rebel. There were angry scenes between Deborah
and her erring son. . . .

But Titus stood his ground. He had paid two
guineas towards the Harvest Fund and he was not
going to pay a penny extra. As for being the chief
opener at the Bazaar he would have nothing
whatever to do with it. . . .

* * *

During another of her unannounced early-
morning visits two days after the Bazaar, Sister
Deborah told Titus of the magnificent performance given by Pa Joel and Simeon at the Bazaar. . . .

'Pa spent money generously—where did he get
it from?' . . .

'It must have been your kinsman then that gave
him the money. Titus, he was simply splen-
did.' . . .

'Mother, I shall tell you something about Simeon my kinsman today. Ever since I came back
I've been trying not to mix my private affairs with
my work. But you and Pa and the whole lot of
you at home have placed me in a very awkward
position.'

'What have we done?'

'Simeon my kinsman. That's what you have
done. Simeon who, according to all of you, is my
kinsman—my brother you call him—is a very bad
man.'

'Ah, Titus! You must ask God for forgiveness.
Why must you sin against an innocent man. You
must pray to God for forgiveness.'

'Simeon is my employee. He is wicked and dis-
honest.'

'Ah, Titus. Everyone knows that he is very
kind. Everyone says so. Pastor too says so. You
must be careful not to say this in the presence of
Pastor.'

'Pastor and the whole Church think that he is
good and kind. That is because he is corrupt. He
steals money from his work. He collects money
from the labourers whom he employs on the
roads. . . . They like him because he gives
plenty of money to the church building fund. It
is all stolen money.'

'Titus, Titus.'

'It is my duty as District Engineer to see that no
one steals any money. It is my duty as District
Engineer to see that no one collects money from
the contractors and workmen. It is therefore my
duty to fight my kinsman Simeon and stop him
from his evil practices.'

'But, Titus,' she cried in stark horror, 'you cannot fight him. He is very strong. He has plenty of
juju. My God, I am lost!' She held her breasts.
She was visibly distressed.

* * *

Titus was unhappy about the Simeon transfer
business in particular, and about Simeon in general. He hated Simeon because of his corruption
and the ineffectiveness of his supervision of his
subordinates. It was his corruption and his ineffi-
ciency that gave the District Officer the chance to
speak to Titus the way he did and the chance of
interfering with his work generally.

It would be a relief if the Foreman were transferred. But as he had explained—to many people
—he was not personally responsible for the trans-

fer, despite the rumours which had filled both
Ibadan and Ibala. . . .

The Rev. Michael Morakinyo prayed for heav-
enly guidance in the crisis that was rapidly en-
gulfing his church. . . .

Apart from the trouble over Simeon Oke's
transfer there was the Bandele vision and the un-
rest it had stirred up among the congregation of
All Souls. . . . Half the Congregation of All
Souls had now come to take Bandele's vision to
mean that the end of the world was imminent and
that it was only a matter of a few weeks or a few
months. . . .

* * *

The following night Simeon went to bed with
an easy mind for the first time for many days, certain that the combined effect of the prayers of
Rev. Morakinyo and his church, the manipula-
tions by the Chief Clerk of the papers in the Provincial Engineer's Office and old Sunmonu's *juju*
would certainly do the trick.

But two days after he was arrested by the Police.

* * *

Deborah was ill.

News of his mother's illness reached Titus in a
note from Pastor Morakinyo and he hurried down
to see her. . . .

'There's something I must tell you, Titus. . . .
Simeon Oke your kinsman was your benefactor.
He was good to your father. He arranged for him
to do the work of a contractor when his trade
went down. . . . That was how he was able to

send money to you to pay for your education in the white man's country. . . . Then he died. . . . And when he died everything became difficult. . . . He gave me the money, I mean your kinsman Simeon. First he gave me £120. Then after you wrote for more money he gave me another £55. Then just before you came back he gave me £60 for my own trading. He told me not to pay back the first £120. But I'm to pay back the £55 and the £60. . . . That's why you must not go to court to give evidence against your kinsman our benefactor.' . . .

For the next few days Titus lived a living death in Ibala. He did his work mechanically. All Ibala now talked of the impending case.

* * *

The prosecution found it difficult to collect evidence against Simeon Oke. . . . No one was willing to come forward to give evidence. . . .

The star witness for the day was Pa Joel. . . .

'You are the father of the family. . . . You must answer the questions precisely, Pa Joel. The big judge does not like you to talk too much.' . . .

The Magistrate was an understanding man and he ruled that the witness should be allowed to say what was in his mind. . . .

'The white man has put you in the position of a big judge and an elder,' he said to His Worship. 'You have wisdom like Solomon, son of David. . . . Both Titus and Simeon are my children. I must not tell lies against either of them. If I do the family god Oluokun will punish me. . . . Titus is not the owner of the farm we are talking about. He has no interest in farms. That is the truth. I think when he went to the white man's country he has read books beyond the point where people are interested in farms. . . . And I want to tell you something. . . . It is a bad thing for people to learn books beyond the point where they are no longer interested in farms.' That again set the whole court rocking with laughter. . . .

Three days after, the Magistrate discharged and acquitted Simeon Oke. . . . He was, however, directing that a formal letter be written to the Director of Public Works bringing to his notice a number of things revealed at the trial which, to his mind, should be the subject of a departmental inquiry under the Public Service Commission Regulations.

* * *

[Titus] wrote to his dear Bola just before going to bed one Saturday night. 'Mother has again been here today. I avoided another row with her. To tell the truth I had neither the strength nor the desire for another row. . . .

Her main argument was that the judge knew everything and if it was true that Simeon committed the crime, he would have known and so sent him to prison. . . . But why should I bore you with these details, when indeed I should be telling you how much I love you and how I am looking forward with mounting excitement to the day when you will come back? . . .

'You won't believe how Bandele has suddenly become important . . . preparing the crowds against the coming of the Lord!

'Yes, you can laugh as much as you like, girl. Of course it must be nonsense. But supposing it

is NOT nonsense—supposing the end of the
world does come in another three and a half
weeks, which is before you come back and before
we get married. Then what becomes of us? . . .
So, my girl, you had better give more thought to
your religious exercises that your own devotion
may save both you and sinful me from the wrath
to come.

'One of the things Mother came to tell me is
that I must go to church tomorrow. It is a special
thanksgiving service, first and foremost for the
discharge and acquittal of Simeon, and secondly
for the restoration of peace in the family, particularly between Simeon and me! Everybody is looking forward to my attending the service. And I've
decided to attend.'

* * *

August 12, the day Judgement Day came to
Ibala, started like any other day. . . .

All around him, Titus noticed that men and
women sang songs of praise. Some recited psalms
. . . 'Allelujah!' . . . 'Father, Father, Father,
Amen.' . . .

Simeon . . . kneeling . . . 'Father, Father,
Father . . . Father of all mercies, I am a miserable sinner . . . I took money from the carpen-
ters and masons that I engaged to work. . . .
For many months I claimed more mileage allowances in respect of my car than I was entitled
to. . . .

'I ask for forgiveness for the lies I told in the
court. . . . The farm was mine. I am sorry to
have lied in court that the farm was not mine. I
ask for God's forgiveness for all my sins.'

Weep Not, Child
James Ngugi

Boro, Kori, and Kamau were all sons of Njeri, Ngotho's eldest wife. Njoroge's only true brother was Mwangi who had died in the war. But they all behaved as if they were of one mother. Kori worked in an African tea-shop called Green Hotel . . . a very popular place because there was a wireless set. . . . Home was especially a nice place when all the brothers and many village girls and boys came in the evening and, sitting around the fireplace in a big circle, they would gossip, laugh and play. . . . But sometimes his brothers did not come. Home then was dull. But the mothers could tell stories. And Ngotho too, when he was in the mood. . . .

It was already dark. While Njeri was always 'our' or 'my elder mother,' Nyokabi, being the younger wife, was always just 'mother.' It was a habit observed and accepted by all. . . .

'Tell us a story. You promised, you know.'

'You children! You never ask your father to tell you stories. Tonight he *will* tell you,' she said smilingly towards her husband. She was happy.

'If you all come to my *Thingira,* I'll tell you one or two.'

From *Weep Not, Child,* © James Ngugi, 1964. Reprinted by permission of Heinemann Educational Books, Ltd.

Njoroge feared his father. But it always made him feel good to listen to him.

* * *

'. . . There was wind and rain. And there was also thunder and terrible lightning. The earth and the forest around Kerinyaga shook. The animals of the forest whom the Creator had recently put there were afraid. There was no sunlight. This went on for many days so that the whole land was in darkness. Because the animals could not move, they just sat and moaned with wind. The plants and trees remained dumb. It was, our elders tell us, all dead except for the thunder, a violence that seemed to strangle life. It was this dark night whose depth you could not measure, not you or I can conceive of its solid blackness, which would not let the sun pierce through it.

'But in this darkness, at the foot of Kerinyaga, a tree rose. At first it was a small tree and grew up, finding a way even through the darkness. It wanted to reach the light, and the sun. This tree had *Life*. It went up, up, sending forth the rich warmth of a blossoming tree—you know a holy tree in the dark night of thunder and moaning. This was Mukuyu, God's tree. Now, you know that at the beginning of things there was only one man (Gikuyu) and one woman (Mumbi). It was under this Mukuyu that he first put them. And immediately the sun rose, and the dark night melted away. The sun shone with a warmth that gave life and activity to all things. The wind and lightning and thunder stopped. The animals stopped wondering and moved. They no longer moaned but gave homage to the Creator and Gi-

kuyu and Mumbi. And the Creator who is also
called Murungu took Gikuyu and Mumbi from
his holy mountain. He took them to the country
of ridges near Siriana and there stood them on a
big ridge before he finally took them to Mukuruwe
wa Gathanga about which you have heard so
much. But he had shown them all the land—yes,
children, God showed Gikuyu and Mumbi all the
land and told them,

> "This land I hand over to you. O Man and
>   woman
> It's yours to rule and till in serenity sacrificing
> Only to me, your God, under my sacred
>   tree . . ."'

There was something strange in Ngotho's eyes. He
looked as if he had forgotten all about those who
were present, Kamau, Njoroge, Boro, Kori, and
many other young men and women who had come
to make the long hours of night shorter by listening to stories. . . . Boro sat in a corner. The expression on his face could not be seen. . . . He
saw fear, gloom and terror of the living things of
the Creator, melting away, touched by the warmth
of the holy tree. . . . The man and woman must
have been blessed to walk in the new Kingdom
with Murungu. He wished he had been there to
stand near Him in His holy place and survey all
the land. Njoroge could not help exclaiming,

> 'Where did the land go?'

Everyone looked at him.

'. . . I am old now. But I too have asked that
question in waking and sleeping. I've said, "What
happened, O Murungu, to the land which you
gave to us? Where, O Creator, went our promised
land?" At times I've wanted to cry or harm my

body to drive away the curse that removed us
from the ancestral lands. I ask, "Have you left
your children naked, O Murungu?"

'I'll tell you. There was a big drought sent to
the land by evil ones who must have been jealous
of the prosperity of the children of the Great One.
But maybe also the children of Mumbi forgot to
burn a sacrifice to Murungu. So he did not shed
His blessed tears that make crops grow. The sun
burnt freely. Plague came to the land. Cattle died
and people shrank in size. Then came the white
man as had long been prophesied by Mugo wa
Kibiro, that Gikuyu seer of old. He came from
the country of ridges, far away from here. Mugo
had told the people of the coming of the white
man. He had warned the tribe. So the white man
came and took the land. But at first not the whole
of it.

'Then came the war. It was the first big war. I
was then young, a mere boy, although circum-
cised. All of us were taken by force. We made
roads and cleared the forest to make it possible
for the warring white man to move more quickly.
The war ended. We were all tired. We came home
worn out but very ready for whatever the British
might give us as a reward. But, more than this,
we wanted to go back to the soil and court it to
yield, to create, not to destroy. But Ng'o! The land
was gone. My father and many others had been
moved from our ancestral lands. He died lonely,
a poor man waiting for the white man to go. Mugo
had said this would come to be. The white man
did not go and he died a *Muhoi* on this very land.
It then belonged to Chahira before he sold it to
Jacobo. I grew up here, but working . . . (here
Ngotho looked all around the silent faces and

then continued) . . . working on the land that
belonged to our ancestors. . . .'

'You mean the land that Howlands farms?'
Boro's voice was cracked, but clear.

'Yes. The same land. My father showed it all
to me. I have worked there too, waiting for the
prophecy to be fulfilled.'

'And do you think it will ever be fulfilled?' It
was Kori who asked this to break the silence that
followed Ngotho's reply.

'I don't know. Once in the country of the ridges
where the hills and ridges lie together like lions, a
man rose. People thought that he was the man
who had been sent to drive away the white man.
But he was killed by wicked people because he
said people should stand together. I've waited for
the prophecy. It may not be fulfilled in my life
time . . . but O, Murungu, I wish it could.' . . .

For Njoroge, it was a surprising revelation,
this knowledge that the land occupied by Mr.
Howlands originally belonged to them.

Boro thought of his father who had fought in
the war only to be dispossessed. He too had gone
to war, against Hitler. He had gone to Egypt, Je-
rusalem and Burma. He had seen things. He had
often escaped death narrowly. But the thing he
could not forget was the death of his stepbrother,
Mwangi. For whom or for what had *he* died?

When the war came to an end, Boro had come
home, no longer a boy but a man with experience
and ideas, only to find that for him there was to be
no employment. There was no land on which he
could settle, even if he had been able to do so. As
he listened to this story, all these things came into
his mind with a growing anger. How could these
people have let the white man occupy the land

without acting? And what was all this superstitious belief in a prophecy?

In a whisper that sounded like a shout, he said, 'To hell with the prophecy.'

Yes, this was nothing more than a whisper. To his father, he said, 'How can you continue working for a man who has taken your land? How can you go on serving him?'

He walked out, without waiting for an answer.

Mine Boy
Peter Abrahams

And the conveyor belt sang and the picks fell and the spades grated and the drills hummed. And everywhere men worked. Their bodies streaming with sweat. . . .

And in Xuma's mind there was room for nothing but his work. Without stopping he would turn his head and call to a man to do this or that or he would warn one who was lingering or he would tell one to leave what he was doing and do something else. And, perhaps, he would look up and catch Paddy's eye, and the Red One would be smiling through his teeth while between them they broke the wall of rock.

And an ever-rising stream of shining rocks and pebbles and fine dust would travel upwards to be sifted, crushed and sorted for the fine yellow metal men love and call gold. . . .

From *Mine Boy*, © 1946 by Peter Abrahams. Reprinted by permission of Alfred A. Knopf, Inc., New York.

One of the men who had been putting up the poles at the weak spot in the tunnel tapped Xuma's shoulder. Xuma stopped his drilling and turned.

'There is water coming through,' the man shouted.

Xuma followed him to the place. He looked up. It was damp and a thin trickle of water seeped through. Xuma called Paddy and showed him the place. Paddy studied it for a little while then went to the phone and shouted for an engineer to come and look at it.

The engineer came down, looked at it, examined it, and said it was safe. Paddy looked at Xuma's face and saw the doubt there. He asked the engineer whether he was certain. The engineer was very firm in his certainty. They went back to their work.

The gold dust streamed upwards to make men wealthy and powerful.

When the hour to eat came the men flung their tools from them and stood around with weariness on their faces and sweat dripping from their bodies. Xuma called them together and told them about the new shifts. Without seeming to care they hurried towards the cages.

A man near Xuma coughed. A trickle of red spittle flew out of his mouth and fell at Xuma's feet. Xuma stared at it. He had heard about the sickness of the lungs and how it ate a man's body away, but he had never seen a man who had it. He looked at the man. The man's eyes shone brightly and his nostrils quivered. He was an old man.

'Come here,' Xuma said.

The man stepped forward. All the others waited and there was fear in their eyes. Xuma felt fear shooting through his body. The man in front of him was still a man. But the signs were there already. He was bony. He was a man who had been big and muscular once and this showed in his boniness.

'You can go,' Xuma said to the others.

They went slowly, reluctantly. When they had gone, Xuma spoke to the man:

'How long have you had this?'

'Two months now,' the man said.

'Did you see the doctor?'

'No,' the man said and hung his head.

'Why not?'

The man looked at the ground and fidgeted with his hands.

'Listen, Xuma, I have a wife and two children and I have worked it all out. We have a small farm and I owe a white man eight pounds. If I do not give it back to him he will take the farm. And if he takes it, where will my wife and children go? I have worked it all out, Xuma, really I have. For four months I have been saving and if I save for another three months I will have the eight pounds and there will be a home for my wife and children. Please let me stay. Don't tell the white people. The others will not. They know. I know I am going to die, but if there is a home for my wife and children I will be happy.'

'And that is why you did not tell of your sickness?'

'That is why.' Xuma felt the fear hammering at his heart.

'What is it, Xuma?'

It was Paddy. He stood a few yards away. Xuma remained silent so Paddy came closer. Paddy looked at the man closely. There was blood at the side of the man's mouth. The man began to cough painfully. Paddy nodded.

'You must see the doctor.'

'No!' the man said.

'Tell him,' Xuma said to the man.

The man told Paddy about his wife and two children and about the eight pounds. When he had finished Paddy turned away and walked to where they had been working. After a little while he came back.

'Did not the man who hired you tell you that if you got the sickness of the chest money would be paid to you?'

'No.'

'Well, it is so,' Paddy said.

The man looked at Xuma. His eagerness was painful.

'Is that so, Xuma?'

Xuma did not know. He looked at Paddy. He hesitated, then nodded.

'Yes, it is so.'

'That is good,' the man said, 'now they will have a home. That is good.'

'Go to the doctor,' Paddy said. 'We will come and everything will be all right.'

The man went. Xuma looked at Paddy.

'Is it true that he will get money?' There was doubt in Xuma's voice.

'Yes, it is true. Come, you will see.' They followed the man into the last cage. The cage shot up. Up. Up. Up.

The other shift was ready and waiting for them. Johannes returned Xuma's key to him. He was quite sober. There were dark rings under his eyes and his hands trembled.

Paddy stood talking to Chris for a minute, then

he called Xuma and they went to the hospital. Xuma waited outside with the man while Paddy went in and spoke to the doctor.

Then the doctor called them in and examined the man. The examination was short. There was no doubt about it. The doctor wrote out a slip and gave it to Paddy.

And again Xuma and the man followed Paddy as he went to the mine manager's office. They waited outside. It seemed a long time. Then the manager came out with Paddy. He grumbled about it being irregular but signed a piece of paper and gave it to Paddy.

'There you are!' Paddy exclaimed. 'Now we will go and get the money and then you can go home.'

The man's lips trembled when he smiled.

They got the money from the cashier. Ten pounds and a full month's wages, three pounds five. That made it thirteen pounds and five shillings. They also got a free railway warrant to the man's home and a pass to show that he was not escaping from the mines. Paddy gave him all this.

'The doctor wants you to go to the hospital but you are also free to go home,' Paddy said.

'Any time?'

'Yes, any time.'

'Even to-day?'

'Yes, even to-day.'

The man clenched his fists to steady himself. He looked at Paddy, then at Xuma and smiled. His eyes shone.

'You are a good man, Red One. And you too, Xuma, you are a real brother. The Great One will look after you. . . . Now there will be a home for my wife and children and I will be with them for a short space. That is good.'

The man saluted them and walked away. The other boys were waiting for him. He told them the good news. And in his joy he pushed out his chest and called out a battle-cry that ended on a painful, lung-tearing cough. The man and his friends joined the column that was going to the compound. It was his last march. Soon he would be with his wife and children. Soon the debt would be paid. . . .

'That was a good thing you did,' Xuma said to Paddy.

'A good thing,' Paddy said bitterly.

Abruptly he walked away and left Xuma standing alone. Xuma stood there for a little while then he went to the wash place. Down the road the tail of the column of marching men disappeared round the bend.

The Gab Boys
Cameron Duodu

I looked round the court-house. I couldn't believe I was on trial. Why, the court looked the same as those countless times when I and other boys went to sit there not because we were particularly interested in how our customary law worked out but because we got quite a few laughs free and we loved our fun. . . .

It was nine o'clock in the morning when the OBK caught me—the time we boys usually boogied up and went to 'town.' So when I arrived

From *The Gab Boys*, copyright © 1967 by Cameron Duodu, reprinted by permission of Andre Deutsch, Ltd., London.

at Kwaa Maanu's shop, the whole pack of lads were there. They sat as usual in the drinking bar adjoining the shop, each with an empty beer bottle and a glass on a table in front of him. . . .

'He can never prove that you did not buy the beer'. . . . So we sat there most mornings and afternoons, discussing the news the paper contained and wondering what the next day's Garth in the *Daily Graphic* would look like.

As soon as I took my seat at one of the tables, I put my hand into my hip pocket and brought out the yellow paper on which the OBK had written my summons, hoping to rock the place with my bit of 'hot' news. But no sooner did the lads see it than they burst out in unison: 'Yieeeeeeeee! . . .'

I was staggered. . . . The boys noticed that I was a bit staggered . . . and without wasting any time, they set the record straight for me—each put his hand in his pocket and brought out a yellow sheet of paper exactly like mine! . . . I felt good now that I knew I was in it with my pals.

The lads gave me the low-down. They had all been dealt with in exactly the same manner as myself—first, the friendly call from the OBK, the moment of suspense, the 'land poll' suddenly thrust at them, and then the 'me-plus-you-come' policemen and their dragging business. . . .

It was Yaw Kyere who hit the nail on the head about why the OBK had declared war on us. . . .

'Friends, Ghanaians, countrymen,' said Yaw Kyere, 'the plain fact, as I see it, is that we Gab Boys are out of favour in this place. When I was passing in front of one of the palm wine bars the other day, I met one of the elders who sit with the chief in his council. This chap looked at my well-

ironed gab trousers and asked me point-blank:
"You people at all, where do you get money to
buy these fine gaberdine trousers?" Of course I
didn't answer him and just looked at him down
my nose. But he went into the palm wine bar,
and one of the maids there . . . said that if I
cared to sit behind the shed on a stone, I would
hear everything they said. . . .

"Look, friends, these boys are getting too many
on our streets. They've finished their schooling
and yet won't go out of town to look for work.
And they won't go to farm with their mothers
and fathers because they say they have been to
school and people who have been to school
shouldn't go to farm any more. They just sit at
home and eat food without producing anything
and yet you see them always well dressed. They're
just a nuisance and if we allow them to go on like
this, they will become a breed of wild worth-
nothings who will just make life impossible for all
of us here".'. . .

It was such 'adventures' that made life worth
living for us.

For to be quite frank, we had nothing else to
live for. We respected nothing and nobody, and
in turn, no one respected us or cared two hoots
about us. . . .

* * *

We Gab Boys of Pusupusu knew that 'corruption' and 'nepotism' meant that the ideal goal of
our society was far from being achieved, so we
resigned ourselves to being *unbeez* and tried to
find as much joy in that sad condition as possible. . . .

However, human nature is not very consistent

and in spite of the casual attitude we took to life, we felt dissatisfied. Deep down, we lacked self-respect. . . .

[It] would be dangerous . . . to ignore our summons and refuse to go to court. That would bring bench warrants against us and as everybody knew, a warrant was a much stronger thing than a summons, for it was nearly always accompanied by handcuffs, and the idea of it should have worried us.

But the talk of warrants had just the opposite effect, for we were in a fighting mood now. . . . 'We won't go to court. Let them bring the warrants.'

I regret to say I was the only one who came out firmly against this idea of not going to court. . . . Any court in the world would acquit us, I foolishly argued. Where on earth were people arrested for not paying taxes when they were known to be unemployed? I asked. Moreover, I added, we were minors; all of us were still in our teens. . . .

Thus it was that I stood in the dock at two o'clock that afternoon. . . . Where were all the other boys who had got summonses like myself? . . . I knew, however, to my great consternation, that the general feeling in the court was against me. . . .

What would She think if She was in court?

They called her simply B, and she was the sauciest honeycomb of a dame you ever saw. . . . She was the daughter of our local Priest and if you have lived in a village like Pusupusu, you will know what that means. Apart from the Chief, no one else commands so much respect as the Priest. In fact, among the christians, he is more respected than the Chief. It is he who baptises their children and gives them 'christian' names which they sometimes find hard to pronounce but which they like all the same—names like Habbakuk or Magdalene—in place of simple Akan names like Kofi and Yaa.

So, my dear B, being of priestly blood, was also really high class. But that was not all. B was a *been-to*—she had gone overseas, to Great Britain. . . .

The spokesman went on: 'You will pay a fine of FIFTEEN POUNDS or go to prison for three months.'. . .

I became woefully frightened. Yieee! Could the world be so cruel? To go to prison and have a criminal's record at the age of nineteen, and that not for any heinous crime like stealing or beating up old women or anything of the sort. Just for not paying land poll when I was unemployed. No, this could not be . . . mustn't be. I MUST ESCAPE! For as surely as the sun rises every day, my mother couldn't borrow fifteen pounds from anybody at Pusupusu on a Monday afternoon like that. And the kind of court we had didn't give anybody time to raise money to pay a fine. . . .

I darted through the door of the OBK's office to the corridor. . . . Boy, I ran ohhh! . . . I decided to wait in the bush until night-fall. . . . By the time I reached the village it was quite dark. . . . I reached B's house. . . . I put my mouth to the window and whispered softly, 'It's me—Small Boy.'. . .

'What will you do when you get to Accra?'. . .

'Oh, I'll loaf around a bit—I've got some taxi-driver friends—afterwards, I'll go to Tema and look for a job.'

'Tema . . . I'll write a note for you'. . . It read:

'Hi Bob,

'This lad is a very good friend of mine . . . who needs a job. Do see him through for me, darling. . . .

I got to Tema safely . . . and sought out the man to whom I had to give B's letter.

I found him in a large air-conditioned office. . . .

'You're Asamoah, eh?' he asked in a lazy but strong voice.

'Yes sir.'

'How's Miss Amoakoa?'

'Very well, sir!'

'When did you arrive?'

'Just half an hour ago.'

'So you want a job, eh? Well, I think we can fix you up.'. . .

'What sort of education do you have?'. . .

'Middle Form Four, sir.'

'Would you like to work on a train?'

'Yes sir; anything.'

'Good. I think we can fix you up.'. . .

* * *

That day was a very lucky day for me, for while we were loading our train with rocks, another train joined us. . . . You could have felled me with a feather when I saw who the fireman on the other train was. It was Kwame Duro, a Pusupusu Gab Boy! . . . Then Kwame and I went aside to have private talks.

'Well, Robin Hood,' Kwame began, 'What a place to meet! I've heard all about you—a lot of the boys came to Takoradi, where I was, to look for work after they'd cleared out.'

'They cleared out?' I asked in surprise.

'Yes, they did. . . . When they heard of your sentence . . . they all vamoosed. . . . Oh, they all ran—Kwadwo Kuma and Yaw Abu came and lodged with me.'. . .

'So what are they doing now?'

'Oh, many have got jobs . . . and there are quite a few in Tema here, though I haven't had time to look for them.'

'Gab Boys here? . . . Oh, we shall be happy here, then.'. . .

'Gee,' he said, 'there's a dance. . . . Like to go?' . . .

'If you want to stay alive here . . . make everybody's business no business of yours and leave the rest to the police.'. . .

Well, how useless all this paper description of music is! Kwame Duro and his girl went crazy; I, sitting alone and listening to the alto-saxist, went crazy and asked a completely strange girl whether she would dance with me. She was willing, but her escort gave me such a look that I said, 'I'm sorry' and left her alone.

* * *

'Wo-o-o-oh! . . . Wo-o-o-o-oh! . . . I woke up . . . I stank; I must have vomited out the entire contents of my stomach. . . . Slowly, the truth dawned on me—I was in a police cell! . . .

So there I stood in the dock again. . . .

'Kwasi Asamoah, you are charged with being drunk and disorderly; do you plead guilty or not guilty?' . . .

'Well, what have you got to say?' the Magistrate asked me.

'Your Worship, I was out with friends at a

dance; I remember putting my head on the table while my friends were dancing; that's all I remember. . . . I believed myself to be in the hands of experienced friends and that I was completely safe; that's why I drank more than I should. I hardly ever drink' . . .

'Five pounds,' said the Magistrate.

I heaved a sigh of relief. . . . I paid the five pounds and left the court. I had no more money with me. . . . I felt like dying right away; I could see myself as others saw me—distraught and unwashed, foul-smelling. . . . There was so much pain in my heart I thought it would burst. Kwame Duro had *left* me in the hands of the police, and had not come back even in the morning to see what they would do with me. . . .

As for the rest of the Gab Boys, I am afraid I didn't give much of a thought to them any longer. *They* had rejected me in my hour of trouble—they'd always had the makings of it but I had loved the idea of *belonging to a group* too much to see that they were individual human beings capable of giving me immense enjoyment . . . but also equipped with the ability to hurt me through sheer stupidity and lack of understanding; through pettiness and betrayal. . . .

Then, I thought, 'Ahaah! Who is a Gab Boy? What is a Gab Boy? Where did you get this idea that there is some group morality to which all should subscribe who have been raised in the same village? . . . Look at the land poll mess. Didn't you stand in the court alone? . . . My boy, this is nothing new at all; people have been speaking about it for years. . .'.

'Oh, but it's painful,' another me, the whining,

subjective one, tried to squash the analysis of the objective one. 'Look,' it said, 'they never tried to understand what happened.'. . .

The objective one replied: 'If somebody had tried to kiss your girl by force, you would have reacted in the same manner.'. . .

'But Kwasi knew me. . . .'

'How do you know whether he thought he knew you? Do you know yourself? Weren't you surprised that *even drunk,* you could behave like that?'

'Yes, probably I thought the girl was B and wanted to kiss her and as I didn't understand why she refused, I tried to force her.'

'Ahaah, would you have thought you could ever force B to do anything she didn't want to do? You see, the drink brought that part of you out. Your selfish, dictatorial self which wants the whole world to become one large Gab Boy world so that you and your Gab Boy friends can roam it laughing and smashing bottles.'. . .

'Everybody knows that drink acts on you *organically;* your brain is affected by the alcohol in your bloodstream and that's how you become unhinged.'

'Unhinged . . . excellent. Can you unhinge something that's not already there? Can you?'. . .

'So, I'm a beast as well as a sane man?'. . .

'God, you've made me afraid of both myself and other men.'. . .

'Listen to you—when did you become a philosopher? . . . So we must bear this philosophy game?'

'As long as we live. Unless we are unthinking fools.'

The Interpreters
Wole Soyinka

Sekoni, qualified engineer, had looked over the railings every day of his sea voyage home. And the sea sprays built him bridges and hospitals, and the large trailing furrow became a deafening waterfall defying human will until he gathered it between his fingers, made the water run in the lower channels of his palm, directing it against the primeval giants on the forest banks. And he closed his palms again, cradling the surge of power. . . .

* * *

Sekoni rushed down the gangway, sought the hand of kindred spirits for the flare of static electricity, but it slipped with grease and pointed to his desk. . . .

'In here. Let me know if there is anything else you need. That is a bell for the messenger.'

Air-conditioned too, Sekoni had no cause for complaint.

'Letters for signature sir . . .'

'If you'd just look over these applications for leave and put up a roster . . .'

'Bicycle advance . . . bicycle advance . . . let me see now, that should be File C/S 429. I'll

From *The Interpreters*, © 1965 by Wole Soyinka. Reprinted by permission of Andre Deutsch, Ltd., London.

check among the B.U.s in the S.M.E.K.'s office. In the meantime will you also take charge of . . .'

'Can I have your contribution sir? For morning tea, or do you prefer to take coffee yourself sir?'

'Please join a preliminary Committee of Five to sort out the applications for the post of a Third Class Clerk. . . .'

'Don't forget the meeting of the Board. You are one of our ex-officio members. . . .'

The fluid rose slowly at that meeting, bursting outside the minutes and agenda of the Board and they all stared, unbelieving.

'You realise, Mr. Sekoni, that you are out of order.'

'I realise, Mmmmister Ch-chairman, that I c-c-cannot conttinue to be ssigning vouchers and llletters and b-b-bicycle allowances . . .'

Pandemonium, except for the practised chairman, calm and full of instant calculations. 'Just wait outside a moment, please, Mr. Sekoni.'

'Is he mad?'

'Omo tani?'

'Why do we employ these too-knows?'

'No, no, no,' and the chairman soothed them. 'He obviously needs a transfer. He's one of the keen ones.'

And to Ijioha Sekoni went, 'where you may work with your hands until your back blisters' and Sekoni built a small experimental power station. And the chairman chuckled and said, 'I knew he was our man. Get me the expat. expert.' Hot from his last lucrative 'evaluation,' came the expatriate expert. Expatriate, therefore impartial.

'Constitute yourself into a one-man commission of enquiry and probe the construction of our

power station at Ijioha which was built without
estimates approved expenditure.'

'Is it unsafe for operation?' and he winked, a
truly expert expat. expert's wink.

'That's the safest idea. You put it in technical
language.'

And the expatriate expert came to Ijioha, saw,
and condemned. . . .

'Interdict him shall we? Bring me Form S2/7
Interdiction of Senior Civil Servants and Confi-
dential File Sekoni Chief Engineer in charge
Ijioha.'

And the chairman—for his subsidiary company
registered in the name of his two-month-old niece
had been sole contractor for Project Ijioha—
cleared out a few thousands in immediate compensation and filed claims for a few thousands
more. 'I always say it, the Write-Offs pay better
than fulfilled contracts.' And to Sekoni, 'the expert says that was junk, Engineer, junk.'

And Sekoni, bewildered, repeating 'J-j-j-junk?
J-j-j-junk . . . ?'

And the papers resounded to 'the escapade of
the mad engineer.'

Sekoni, obscuring himself in the streets of
Ibadan, . . . waiting for a decision to be taken
on his fate by the next meeting of the governing
board. Hearing often the whirr of motors that he
had built, the assemblage of a million parts that
he had scavenged touring the various stations
under his command more like a junk-cart than as
a Senior Civil Engineer in charge, prodding
crumpled heaps of motor cars and lorries, trac-
tors, railway yards, scrounging. . . .

'J-j-j-junk?' The Chairman had called it junk.
And the plant had never even been tested! Bigger
towns still worked their refrigerators by kerosene,

but Sekoni's plant would bathe Ijioha maidens in neon glow—the Village Head had chuckled at that, and Sekoni, carried forward on the excitement, began plans for a waterworks, to be constructed as soon as the power station was finished. Incredulous on his observation perch, the Head had promised him three wives, to include his own daughter.

And this the chairman had called it 'J-j-j-junk!' When the furnace had never even been lit!

* * *

At Ijioha the weeds were reaching high among the baked brick huts of the power plant. . . . The silence descended round him, of a grass snake coiled beside a plastered ledge, of buckets rusting on conveyor cables. Following them he came to the tipping device which knocked the coal into a chute and led straight into the furnace. He had been rather proud of that. He walked towards the control chamber. There were new bolts on the door beside the lock, and on the wall someone had splashed in whitewash—DANGEROUS. KEEP OFF in two languages. He looked round for a heavy object, found a large stone and stooped to pick it.

'Oh, so it was you, Engineer.'

Sekoni spun round, came face to face with the village Head.

'Did I scare you? Some children came and told me of a stranger prowling round the place. So I thought I would come up and see.'

Stranger! It was only two months. Sekoni knew those children, and they must have remembered him. The Head appeared to sense what he was thinking. 'It must have been your beard. You didn't have that when you were here.'

His hand moved involuntarily to his chin, scraping the beard with the back of his hand. He had forgotten about that, no, it was more accurate to say he had never really been conscious of it. And he began to think of it like a new problem, some cause for a decision, amazed that he had never really noticed it sprout.

The Head looked at him with some apprehension, and seemed to feel his way around the engineer. Something he could not quite decide, and it urged him to be wary.

'You didn't even come back to say good-bye to us.'

'I . . . I . . . have cccome back.'

'Oh yes, oh yes. There are many people who still talk of you.'

'I-er . . . I came to t-t-test the plant.'

At first the Head did not believe he heard right. He looked at him in doubt, pointed towards the plant. Sekoni nodded, as if in confidence.

The Head put it in words. 'You want to get this thing going?'

More eagerly, Sekoni nodded. 'Th-they say it c-c-can't work, b-b-but th-that is all rrrubbish.'

The Chief's hostility was now unmistakable. 'They don't say it won't work. It will not only work, it will blow up. It will blow up and blow up the village with it.'

Sekoni became incoherent, a throbbing vein out on his forehead and his neck-muscles working with self-destructive strength. 'D-d-don't believe it. D-d-d-don't bbbelieve it. If ththey only allowed me to tttest . . .'

'If you want to test it, my friend, just uproot your funny thing and carry it with you. Go and test it in the bush, or in your home town. Electricity is government thing, we all know that. The white men know about it, and one came here and told us. They know what they are talking about.'

'Lllies. Lllies. The-they c-c-called it jjunk. Jjjunk! And ththat man even came here without my p-p-plans.'

'Look, take my advice, just go back before more people see you.' . . .

'One lllload from every ch-ch-child, th-then you will see it work. If yyyou find me the wood, you will s-s-see lllight g-g-glowing from th-that post.'

'Thank you very much. We've used oil-lamps until now. When government is ready, they will build us a proper one.'

'Only one t-t-test. You have to sssee for your . . . self.'

'Come now, before people begin to gather . . .' And as he placed a hand on Sekoni's arm, Sekoni broke suddenly loose and seized the boulder. The Head screamed for help and fled, not even looking round to see Sekoni who had begun to batter the door. It flew away from the lock and the bolts and the reinforcement of six-inch nails. When the chief returned with help, they found Sekoni oiling the machines and inspecting the meters. He turned round, seeing the chief and asked, 'Have you brought the firewood?'

* * *

Surprisingly, he had allowed the police to lead him off without resistance. There was another Commission of Enquiry, but by then Sekoni lay in a mental hospital.

* * *

And the vows of silence. Above all else, the vows of silence must be kept. Against love, against need and the willingness to give. And re-

morse proved powerless against such silence as
bound Sekoni's father to a silent distance until
death. A Christian girl! This sin, so heinous, so
unfilial and blasphemous, no longer seared the
memory of Alhaji Sekoni, but a vow was a vow,
and pride propped his thirsted flesh when it
would want to fall to love. Five years ago he had
stood at the door of the Marriage Registry and
implored the wrath of hurricanoes on the treachery of his blood, his *haji* mantle blown about his
shoulders like the name of Lear on an asphalt
heath. And his desolation equally felt, equally
unsolved. 'I will never, never open my mouth to
speak to you. May Allah in his might strike me
dead if I speak another word to you!'

And now bearing a stiff, manful back down on
the pangs of separation, Alhaji Sekoni, nearly
demented himself with grief and worry, made a
home on the doorstep of the doctor. How is he,
sir, tell me how is he? Will he recover? And remember that nothing need be lacking. If you want
to send him abroad to specialists . . . no? Don't
they say Switzerland has the best of everything?
But doctor, surely there is something I can do,
there is something I must do? What does he talk
about? And who does he talk about? He mentions
names? No no I only wondered . . . has he
stated a desire to see anyone in particular? Did
you say no? Only I hear that often they desire to
see someone or other. There is a nurse with him
all the time? But there ought to be . . . it will be
so bad if he wants to see one of his er friends or
. . . er relations, and we don't know anything
about it . . . no no, he has no brothers or sisters
. . . well, if there is anything at all, maybe a
change of air, you are the doctor, what do you

think? A change of air, a holiday is always good, isn't it?

The doctor understood whose need this truly was and the elder patient left then, already on the way to recovery. . . .

* * *

The rains of May become in July slit arteries of the sacrificial bull, a million bleeding punctures of the sky-bull hidden in convulsive cloud humps, black, overfed for this one event, nourished on horizon tops of endless choice grazing, distant beyond giraffe reach. Some competition there is below, as bridges yield right of way to lorries packed to the running-board, and the wet tar spins mirages of unspeed-limits to heroic cars and their cargoes find a haven below the precipice. The blood of earth-dwellers mingles with blanched streams of the mocking bull, and flows into currents eternally below earth. The Dome cracked above Sekoni's short-sighted head one messy night. Too late he saw the insanity of a lorry parked right in his path, a swerve turned into a skid and cruel arabesques of tyres. A futile heap of metal, and Sekoni's body lay surprised across the open door, showers of laminated glass around him, his beard one fastness of blood and wet earth.

It helped Egbo not at all that he fled to the rocks by the bridge until the funeral was over where unseen he shed his bitter angry tears, or Sagoe locked in beer and vomit for a week and Dehinwa despairing of his temperature, battling to keep him quiet while he bawled you're wetting me all over with your goddam tears. And he would only rest when she agreed to retrieve his

Books of Enlightenment and read to him from a
random page. . . .

* * *

To Bandele fell the agony of consoling Alhaji
Sekoni, his vow violently cancelled for ever. . . .

And Kola's brush raised itself again and again,
faltered and worked blindly in spasms of grief
and unbelieving. . . .

* * *

A fortnight after the funeral they all met again,
listening listlessly to another group of wandering
players and the long wail of a horse-tail bow on a
string and a sound-box of calabash. . . .

* * *

Sekoni's death had left them all wet, bedraggled, the paint running down their acceptance of
life where they thought the image was set, running
down in ugly patches. . . .

race

Ethnocentrism—belief in the superiority of one's own ethnic group—was as strong in pre-colonial Africa as in the rest of the world.

But racism, an especially virulent form of group hatred, was introduced to Africa by white Europeans during the colonial period. Racism has been an inescapable fact of life for the black African ever since.

A variety of social structures can be devised to carry out racist practices. (1) The racist can annihilate the hated group. Whites have practically annihilated several African ethnic (tribal) groups. (2) The racist can segregate the hated group. Colonialists walled themselves off into plush reserves in African cities. In South Africa the "grand design" in race relations is apartheid: regional residential segregation. (3) The racist can stratify the hated group, placing his own group at the top and the detested group at the bottom. In East, Central and Southern colonial Africa, society was composed of layers: whites on top, Asians in the middle and Africans on the

bottom. *In South Africa today there are layers of
whites: Afrikaner-Christians on top, followed by
English-Christians, then Jews. Following in de-
scending order are Asians, coloreds and black
Africans.*

*Equalitarianism can be organized into at least
two structures. (1) Races can integrate. In the
U.S.A. there is a struggle to bring about educational, residential and occupational integration.
(2) Races can "live and let live" in a structured
pluralism, in which different races and ethnic
groups preserve their own cultural heritages
within a unified government, which represents
all and plans for all. In Canada there is a struggle
to strengthen pluralistic structures between two
ethnic groups, French and English. Switzerland
has united four language groups pluralistically:
Italian, French, German and Romansch. Where
racial differences are added to cultural differences,
the challenge to make a democratic pluralism
work is intensified.*

*In Africa equalitarianism between races has
been smothered. Integration is difficult because
both racism and reverse racism exist. Pluralism
in Africa has not succeeded either: groups that
should have been organized as co-equals have
always been stratified, and governments that
should have been concerned equally for the welfare of each group have invariably given excessive
privileges to whites and withheld them all from
blacks.*

*The selections in this chapter illustrate several
specific effects of racism.*

The story of the Houseboy *by Oyono takes
place in the Camerouns during French colonial
rule. The young black servant of a white com-*

mandant is forced to watch the white prison guard order the prolonged, agonizing death of two African suspects. The story shows that racism is brutal.

The poem, "Telephone Conversation," by Wole Soyinka, could take place anywhere in Europe or America—the author does not tell us where. An African student abroad is hunting for a room to live in. To save disappointment he calls a prospective landlady. Her response shows how racism cheapens life.

In Papa, the Snake and I, an African writer from Portuguese Mozambique, Luis Bernardo Honwana, describes Mr. Castro as an arrogant local white man who bosses an "assimilated" African father and his family who come from the Ronga ethnic (tribal) group. It is very difficult for a father to be a man to his son when he docilely obeys a bully's every demand. Racism injures family relationships.

In "The Park," by James Matthews, a little South African colored boy wants more than anything else to play on a white playground. When he is thrown out, he asks himself, with a misplaced sense of guilt, "What have I done wrong?" He has done nothing wrong. Racism hurts the self-image of the one discriminated against.

In the same story a white lady prefers to feed scraps of food to this little boy than to pay his mother decent wages for doing her family's laundry by hand. Institutionalized racism can exist hand in hand with sentimentalized generosity.

A university-educated white Afrikaner named Stoffel is preparing a Commission report for the government of South Africa in Ezekiel Mphahlele's short story, "The Living and the Dead." In

the report he advocates that almost all black
servants be prohibited from living in the servant
quarters of white suburbs and be forced to com-
mute many miles each day. In this story Jackson
and his wife, Virginia, are such servants working
and living separately as required by law for two
different "masters" in two different suburbs.
Mphahlele asks: "Who is alive and who is already
dead?" If the essence of life is love, there is no
life in Stoffel. Racism destroys the one who hates.

Houseboy
Ferdinand Oyono

My master is off into the bush again this morning. He is indefatigable. I am frightened. It makes
things very awkward for me. While he was here I
had some security. What has Madame got up her
sleeve? She says nothing. She won't even call me
by name. She just signals. She signalled me to
come this morning when she gave me the letter. I
had to take it to her lover as soon as her husband
had gone.

The prison-director was busy with two Africans
suspected of stealing from M. Janopoulos. He
was 'teaching them how to behave.'

With the help of a constable he was giving
them a flogging in front of M. Janopoulos. They
were stripped to the waist and handcuffed. There
was a rope round their necks, tied to the pole in

From *Houseboy*, by Ferdinand Oyono. Copyright ©
1966 by John Reed (for translation). Reprinted by permission of the Macmillan Company, New York.

the Flogging Yard, so that they couldn't turn their necks towards the blows.

It was terrible. The hippopotamus-hide whip tore up their flesh. Every time they groaned it went through my bowels. M. Moreau with his hair down over his face and his shirt sleeves rolled up was setting about them so violently that I wondered, in agony of mind, if they would come out of it alive. Chewing on his cigar M. Janopoulos released his dog. It mouthed about the heels of the prisoners and tore at their trousers.

'Confess, you thieves,' shouted M. Moreau. 'Give them the butt of your rifle, Ndjangoula.'

The huge Sara ran up, presented his weapon and brought down the butt on the suspects.

'Not on the head, Ndjangoula, they've got hard heads. In the kidneys.'

Ndjangoula brought the butt down on their kidneys. They went down, got up and then went down again under another violent blow to the kidneys.

Janopoulos was laughing. M. Moreau panted for breath. The prisoners had lost consciousness.

M. Moreau is right, we must have hard heads. When Ndjangoula brought down his rifle butt the first time, I thought their skulls would shatter. I could not hold myself from shaking as I watched. It was terrible. I thought of all the priests, all the pastors, all the white men, who come to save our souls and preach love of our neighbours. Is the white man's neighbour only other white men? Who can go on believing the stuff we are served up in the churches when things happen like I saw today . . .

It will be the usual thing. M. Moreau's suspects will be sent to the 'Blackman's Grave' where they will spend a few days painfully dying. Then they

will be buried naked in the prisoners' cemetery.
On Sunday, the priest will say, 'Dearly beloved
brethren, pray for all those prisoners who die
without making their peace with God.' M. Moreau
will present his upturned topee to the faithful.
Everyone will put in a little more than he had in-
tended. All the money goes to the whites. They
are always thinking up new ways to get back what
little money they pay us.

How wretched we are.

Telephone Conversation
Wole Soyinka

The price seemed reasonable, location
Indifferent. The landlady swore she lived
Off premises. Nothing remained
But self-confession. 'Madam,' I warned,
'I hate a wasted journey—I am—African.'
Silence. Silenced transmission of
Pressurized good-breeding. Voice, when it came,
Lip-stick coated, long gold-rolled
Cigarette-holder pipped. Caught I was, foully.
'HOW DARK?' . . . I had not misheard . . . 'ARE
    YOU LIGHT
OR VERY DARK?' Button B. Button A. Stench
Of rancid breath of public-hide-and-speak.
Red booth. Red pillar-box. Red double-tiered
Omnibus squelching tar. It *was* real! Shamed
By ill-mannered silence, surrender
Pushed dumbfoundment to beg simplification.

From *A Book of African Verse*, John Reed and Clive
Wake (eds.). Reprinted by permission of Heinemann
Educational Books, Ltd.

Considerate she was, varying the emphasis—
'ARE YOU DARK? OR VERY LIGHT?' Revelation
   came.
'You mean—like plain or milk chocolate?'
Her assent was clinical, crushing in its light
Impersonality. Rapidly, wave-length adjusted,
I chose, 'West African sepia'—and as an after-
   thought,
'Down in my passport.' Silence for spectroscopic
Flight of fancy, till truthfulness clanged her accent
Hard on the mouthpiece. 'WHAT'S THAT?' conced-
   ing
'DON'T KNOW WHAT THAT IS.' 'Like brunette.'
'THAT'S DARK, ISN'T IT?' 'Not altogether.
'Facially, I am brunette, but madam, you should
   see
The rest of me. Palm of my hand, soles of my feet
Are a peroxide blond. Friction, caused—
Foolishly madam—by sitting down, has turned
My bottom raven black—One moment madam!'
   —sensing
Her receiver rearing on the thunder clap
About my ears—'Madam,' I pleaded, 'Wouldn't
   you rather
See for yourself?'

Papa, the Snake and I
Luis Bernardo Honwana

The distance between the snake and the dog
was about five feet. However, the snake had in-

From *We Killed Mangy-Dog,* © by Luis Bernardo
Honwana. Reprinted by permission of A. P. Watt &
Son, London.

serted its tail in the angle formed between a block
and the ground, and had raised its coils one by
one, preparing for the strike. The triangular head
drew back imperceptibly, and the base of the
lifted neck came forward. Seeming to be aware of
the proximity of his end, the dog began to bark
even more frantically, without, however, trying to
get away from the snake. From a little way behind, Toto, now on his feet as well, joined in the
barking.

For a fraction of a second the neck of the snake
curved while the head leaned back. Then, as if
the tension of its pliant body had snapped a cord
that fastened its head to the ground, it shot forward in a lightning movement impossible to follow. Although the dog had raised himself on his
hind legs like a goat, the snake struck him full on
the chest. Free of support, the tail of the snake
whipped through the air, reverberating with the
movement of the last coil.

Wolf fell on his back with a suppressed whine,
pawing convulsively. The mamba abandoned him
immediately, and with a spring disappeared between the pipes.

'A Nhoka!' screamed Sartina.

Nandito threw me aside and ran out of the
chicken run with a yell, collapsing into the arms
of Madunana. As soon as he felt free of the snake,
Wolf vanished in half a dozen leaps in the direction of Mr. Castro's house.

The children all started to cry without having
understood what had happened. Sartina took
Nandito to the house, carrying him in her arms.
Only when the children disappeared behind Sartina did I call Madunana to help me kill the snake.

Madunana waited with a cloth held up high
while I moved the pipes with the aid of a broom-

stick. As soon as the snake appeared Madunana threw the cloth over it, and I set to beating the heap with my stick.

* * *

When Papa came back from work Nandito had come round from the shock, and was weeping copiously. Mama, who had not yet been to see the snake, went with Papa to the chicken run. I went there as well, and saw Papa turn the snake over on its back with a stick.

'I don't like to think of what a snake like this could have done to one of my children,' Papa smiled. 'Or to anyone else. It was better this way. What hurts me is to think that these six feet of snake were attained at the expense of my chickens. . . .'

At this point Mr. Castro's car drew up in front of our house. Papa walked up to him, and Mama went to talk to Sartina. I followed after Papa.

'Good afternoon, Mr. Castro. . . .'

'Listen, Tchembene, I've just found out that my pointer is dead, and his chest's all swollen. My natives tell me that he came howling from your house before he died. I don't want any back-chat, and I'm just telling you—either you pay compensation or I'll make a complaint at the Administration. He was the best pointer I ever had.'

'I've just come back from work—I don't know anything . . .'

'I don't care a damn about that. Don't argue. Are you going to pay or aren't you?'

'But, Mr. Castro . . .'

'Mr. Castro nothing. It's eight pounds. And it's better if the matter rests here.'

'As you like, Mr. Castro, but I don't have the money now. . . '

'We'll see about that later. I'll wait until the end of the month, and if you don't pay then there'll be a row.'

'Mr. Castro, we've known each other such a long time, and there's never . . .'

'Don't try that with me. I know what you all need—a bloody good hiding is the only thing. . . .'

Mr. Castro climbed into his car and pulled away. Papa stayed watching while the car drove off. 'Son of a bitch. . . .'

I went up to him, and tugged at the sleeve of his coat.

'Papa, why didn't you say that to his face?'

He didn't answer.

* * *

We had hardly finished supper when Papa said, 'Mother, tell Sartina to clear the table quickly. My children, let us pray. Today we are not going to read the Bible. We will simply pray.'

Papa talked in Ronga, and for this reason I regretted having asked him that question a while ago.

When Sartina finished clearing away the plates and folded the cloth, Papa began, 'Tatana, ha ku dumba hosi ya tilo ni misaba . . .'

When he finished, his eyes were red.

Amen!

Amen!

Mama got up, and asked, as if it meant nothing, 'But what did Mr. Castro want, after all?'

'It's nothing important.'

'All right, tell me about it in our room. I'll go

and set out the children's things. You, Ginho, wake up early tomorrow and take a laxative. . . .'

When they had all gone away, I asked Papa, 'Papa, why do you always pray when you are very angry?'

'Because He is the best counsellor.'

'And what counsel does He give you?'

'He gives me no counsel. He gives me strength to continue.'

'Papa, do you believe a lot in Him?'

Papa looked at me as if he were seeing me for the first time, and then exploded, 'My son, one must have a hope. When one comes to the end of a day, and one knows that tomorrow will be another day just like it, and that things will always be the same, we have got to find the strength to keep on smiling, and keep on saying, "This is not important!" We ourselves have to allot our own reward for all the heroism of every day. We have to establish a date for this reward, even if it's the day of our death! Even today you saw Mr. Castro humiliate me: this formed only part of today's portion, because there were many things that happened that you didn't see. No, my son, there must be a hope! It must exist! Even if all this only denies Him, He must exist!'

Papa stopped suddenly, and forced himself to smile. Then he added, 'Even a poor man has to have something. Even if it is only a hope! Even if it's a false hope!'

'Papa, I could have prevented the snake from biting Mr.Castro's dog. . . .'

Papa looked at me with his eyes full of tenderness, and said under his breath, 'It doesn't matter. It's a good thing that he got bitten.'

Mama appeared at the door. 'Are you going to let the child go to sleep or not?'

I looked at Papa, and we remembered Mr. Castro and both of us burst out laughing. Mama didn't understand.

'Are you two going crazy?'

'Yes, and it's about time we went crazy,' said Papa with a smile.

Papa was already on the way to his room, but I must have talked too loudly. Anyway, it was better that he heard, 'Papa, I sometimes . . . I don't really know . . . but for some time . . . I have been thinking that I didn't love you all. I'm sorry. . . .'

Mama didn't understand what we had been saying, so she became angry. 'Stop all this, or else . . .'

'Do you know, my son,' Papa spoke ponderously, and gesticulated a lot before every word. 'The most difficult thing to bear is that feeling of complete emptiness . . . and one suffers very much . . . very, very, very much. One grows with so much bottled up inside, but afterwards it is difficult to scream, you know.'

The Park
James Matthews

He looked longingly at the children on the other side of the railings; the children sliding down the

From *Quartet: New Voices from South Africa*. Reprinted by permission of Crown Publishers, Inc.

chute, landing with feet astride on the bouncy lawn; screaming as they almost touched the sky with each upward curve of their swings; their joyful, demented shrieks at each dip of the merry-go-round. He looked at them and his body trembled and itched to share their joy—buttocks to fit board, and hands and feet to touch steel. Next to him, on the ground, was a bundle of clothing, washed and ironed, wrapped in a sheet.

Five small boys, pursued by two bigger ones, ran past, ignoring him. One of the bigger boys stopped. 'What are you looking at, you brown ape?' he said, stooping to pick up a lump of clay. He recognized him. The boy was present the day he was put out of the park. The boy pitched the lump, shattering it on the rail above his head and the fragments fell on his face.

He spat out the particles of clay clinging to the lining of his lips, eyes searching for an object to throw at the boys separated from him by the railings. More boys joined the one in front of him and he was frightened by their number.

Without a word he shook his bundle free from the clay and raised it to his head and walked away.

As he walked he recalled his last visit to the park. Without hesitation he had gone through the gates and got on to the nearest swing. Even now he could feel that pleasurable thrill which travelled the length of his body as he rocketed himself higher, higher, until he felt that the swing would up-end him when it reached its peak. Almost leisurely he had allowed it to come to a halt, like a pendulum shortening its stroke, and then ran towards the see-saw. A white boy, about his own age, was seated opposite him. Accordion-like,

their legs folded to send the see-saw jerking from
the indentation it pounded in the grass. A hand
pressing on his shoulder stopped a jerk. He turned
around to look into the face of the attendant.

'Get off!' The skin tightened between his eyes.
'Why must I get off? What have I done?' He held
on, hands clamped on to the iron hoop attached to
the wooden see-saw. The white boy jumped off
from the other end and stood—a detached spec-
tator. 'You must get off!' The attendant spoke in a
low voice so that it would not carry to the people
who were gathering.

'The council says,' he continued, 'that we col-
oureds must not use the same swings as the whites.
You must use the park where you stay.' His voice
apologizing for the uniform he wore which gave
him the right to be in the park to watch that the
little whites were not hurt while playing.

'There's no park where we stay.' He waved a
hand in the direction of a block of flats. 'There's
a park on the other side of town but I don't know
where it is.' He walked past them. The mothers
with their babies—pink and belching—cradled in
their arms, the children lolling on the grass, his
companion from the see-saw, the nurse girls—
their uniforms their badges of indemnity—pushing prams. Beside him walked the attendant. At
the entrance, the attendant pointed an accusing
finger at a notice board.

'There you can read for yourself.' Absolving
himself of any blame. He struggled with the red
letters on the white background.

'Blankes Alleen, Whites Only.' He walked
through the gates and behind him the swings
screeched, the see-saw rattled, and the merry-go-
round rumbled.

He walked past the park as on each occasion after that he had been forced to walk past it.

He shifted the bundle to a more comfortable position, easing the pain biting into his shoulder muscles. What harm would I be doing if I were to use the swings? Would it stop the swings from swinging? Would the chute collapse? The bundle pressed deeper and the pain became an even line across his shoulders and he had no answer to his reasoning.

The park itself, with its wide lawns and flower-beds and rockeries and dwarf trees, meant noth-ing to him. It was the gaily painted tubing, the silver chains and brown boards, transport to never-never land, which gripped him.

Only once, long ago, and then almost as if by mistake, had he been on something to beat it. He was taken by his father, in one of those rare mo-ments when they were taken anywhere, to a fair ground. He had stood captivated by the wooden horses with their gilded reins and scarlet saddles dipping in time to the music as they whirled by.

For a brief moment he was astride one and he prayed it would last for ever, but the moment lasted only the time it took him to whisper the prayer. Then he was standing, clutching his fa-ther's trousers, watching the other riders astride the dipping horses.

Another shifting of the bundle and he was at the house where he delivered the clothing his mother had washed in a round tub, filled with boiling water, the steam covering her face with a film of sweat. Her voice, when she spoke, was as soft and clinging as the steam enveloping her.

He pushed the gate open and walked around the back, watching for the aged lap-dog which, at

his entry, would rush out to wheeze asthmatically
around his feet and nip with blunt teeth at his
ankles.

A round-faced African girl, her blackness
heightened by the white, starched uniform she
wore, opened the kitchen door to let him in. She
cleared the table and placed the bundle on it.

'I will call madam.' She said the words spaced
and highly pitched as if she had some difficulty in
uttering the syllables in English. Her buttocks
bounced beneath the tight uniform and the backs
of her calves shone with fat.

'Are you sure you've brought everything?' was
the greeting he received each time he brought the
bundle, and each time she checked every item and
always nothing was missing. He looked at her and
lowered his voice as he said, 'Everything's there,
madam.'

What followed had become a routine between
the three of them.

'Have you had anything to eat?' she asked him.

He shook his head.

'Well, we can't let you go off like that.' Turn-
ing to the African woman in the white, starched
uniform, 'What have we got?'

The maid swung open the refrigerator door and
took out a plate of food. She placed it on the table
and set a glass of milk next to it.

When he was seated the white woman left the
kitchen and he was alone with the maid.

His nervousness left him and he could concen-
trate on what was on the plate.

A handful of peas, a dab of mashed potato, a
tomato sliced into bleeding circles, a sprinkling of
grated carrots, and no rice.

White people are funny, he told himself. How

can anyone fill himself with this? It doesn't form a lump, like the food my mama makes.

He washed it down with milk.

'Thank you, Annie,' he said as he pushed the glass aside.

Her teeth gleamed porcelain-white as she smiled.

He sat fidgeting, impatient to be outside, away from the kitchen with its glossy, tiled floor and steel cupboards Duco-ed a clinical white to match the food-stacked refrigerator.

'I see you have finished.' The voice startled him. She held out an envelope containing the ten-shilling note—payment for his mother's weekly struggle over the wash tub. 'This is for you.' A sixpence was dropped into his hand, a long fingernail raking his palm.

'Thank you, madam.' His voice barely audible.

'Tell your mother I'm going away on holiday for about a month and I will let her know when I'm back.'

Then he was dismissed and her high heels tapped out of the kitchen. He nodded his head at the African maid who took an apple from the bowl which was bursting with fruit, and handed it to him.

Her smile bathed her face in light.

As he walked down the path he finished off the apple with big bites.

Before he reached the gate the dog was after him, its hot breath warming his heels. He turned and poked his toes into its face. It barked hoarsely in protest, a look of outrage on its face.

He laughed delightedly at the expression which changed the dog's features into those of an old man.

Let's see you do that again. He waved his foot in front of the pug-nose. The nose retreated and made an about-turn, waddling away with its dignity deflated by his affront.

As he walked he mentally spent his sixpence.

I'll buy a penny drops, the sour ones which taste like limes; a penny bull's eyes, a packet of sherbet with the licorice tube at the end of the packet; and a penny star toffees, red ones, which colour your tongue and turn your spittle into blood.

His glands were titillated and his mouth filled with saliva. He stopped at the first stop and walked inside.

Trays were filled with expensive chocolates and sweets of a type never seen in jars on the shelves of the Indian shop at the corner where he stayed. He walked out, not buying a thing.

His footsteps lagged as he reached the park.

The nurse girls with their babies and prams were gone, their places occupied by old men, who, with their hands holding up their stomachs, were casting disapproving eyes over the confusion and clatter confronting them.

A ball was kicked perilously close to one old man, and the boy who ran after it stopped as the old man raised his stick, daring him to come closer.

The rest of them called to the boy to get the ball. He edged closer and made a grab at it as the old man swung his cane. The cane missed him by more than a foot and he swaggered back, the ball held under his arm. Their game was resumed.

From the other side of the railings he watched them; the boys kicking the ball; the children cavorting on the grass; even the old men, senile on the seats; but most of all, the children enjoying themselves with what was denied him; and his whole body yearned to be part of them.

'Damn it!' He looked over his shoulder to see if anyone had heard him. 'Damn it!' he said louder. 'Damn on them! Their park, the grass, the swings, the see-saw. Everything! Damn it! Damn it!'

His small hands impotently shook the tall railings towering above his head.

It struck him that he would not be seeing the park for a whole month, that there would be no reason for him to pass it.

Despair filled him. He had to do something to ease his anger.

A bag filled with fruit peelings was on top of the rubbish stacked in a waste-basket fitted to a pole. He reached for it and frantically threw it over the railings. He ran without waiting to see the result.

Out of breath three streets farther, he slowed down, pain stabbing beneath his heart. The act had brought no relief, only intensified the longing.

He was oblivious of the people passing, the hoots of the vehicles whose path he crossed without thinking. Once, when he was roughly pushed aside, he did not even bother to look and see who had done it.

The familiar shrieks and smells told him he was home.

The Indian shop could not draw him out of his melancholy mood and he walked past it, his sixpence unspent, in his pocket.

A group of boys were playing on the pavement.

Some of them called to him but he ignored them and turned into a short side-street.

He mounted the flat stoep of a double-storey house with a facade that must have been painted once but had now turned a nondescript grey with the red brick underneath showing through.

Beyond the threshold the room was dim. He walked past the scattered furniture with a familiarity that did not need guidance.

His mother was in the kitchen, hovering above a pot perched on a pressure stove.

He placed the envelope on the table. She put aside the spoon and stuck a finger under the flap of the envelope, tearing it in half. She placed the ten-shilling note in a spoutless teapot on the shelf.

'Are you hungry?'

He nodded his head.

She poured him a cup of soup and added a thick slice of brown bread.

Between bites of bread and sips of the soup which scalded his throat he told her that there wouldn't be any washing coming during the week.

'Why? What's the matter? What have I done?'

'Nothing. Madam says she's going away for a month and she'll let mama know when she gets back.'

'What am I going to do now?' Her voice took on a whine and her eyes strayed to the teapot containing the money. The whine hardened to reproach as she continued. 'Why didn't she let me know she was going away? I could have looked for another madam.'

She paused. 'I slave away and the pain never leaves my back, and it's too much for her to let me know she's going away. The money I get from her just keeps us nicely steady. How am I going to cover the hole?'

As he ate, he wondered how the ten shillings he

had brought helped to keep them nicely steady.
There was no change in their meals. It was, as
usual, not enough and the only time they received
new clothes was at Christmas.

'There's the burial to pay and I was going to
ask Mr. Lemonsky to bring some lino for the front
room. I'm sick of seeing boards where the lino's
worn through, but it's no use asking him to bring
it now. Without money you have as much hope as
getting wine on a Saturday.'

He hurried his eating to get away from the
words wafting towards him, before they could
soak into him, trapping him in the chair to witness
his mother's miseries.

Outside, they were still playing with their tyres.
He joined them half-heartedly. As he rolled the
tyre, his spirit was in the park on the swings.
There was no barrier to his coming and he could
do as he pleased. He was away from the narrow
streets and squawking children and speeding cars.
He was in a place of green grass and red tubing
and silver steel. The tyre rolled past him. He
made no effort to grab it.

'Go get the tyre.'. . . 'Are you asleep?'. . .
'Don't you want to play any more?' He walked
away, ignoring their cries.

Rage boiled up inside him. Rage against the
houses with their streaked walls and smashed
panes filled by too many people; the overflowing
garbage pails outside doors; the alleys and streets;
and a law he could not understand; a law that shut
him out of the park.

He burst into tears. He swept his arms across
his cheeks to check his weeping.

He lowered his hands to peer at the boy confronting him.

'I'm not crying, damn you. Something's gone into my eye and I was rubbing it.'

'I think you're crying.'

He pushed past and continued towards the shop. 'Crying doll!' the boy's taunt rang after him.

The shop's sole, iron-barred window was crowded. Oranges were mixed with writing paper and dried figs were strewn on school slates; clothing and crockery collected dust. Across the window a cockroach made its leisurely way, antennae on the alert.

Inside, the shop was as crowded as the window. Bags covered the floor, leaving a narrow path to the counter. 'Yes, boy?' He showed teeth scarlet with betel.

'Come'n, boy. What you want? No stand here all day.' His jaws worked at the betel-nut held captive by his stained teeth.

He ordered penny portions of his selections.

Transferring the sweets to his pocket he threw the torn container on the floor and walked out. Behind him the Indian murmured grimly, jaws working faster.

One side of the street was in shadow. He sat with his back against the wall, savouring the last of the sun.

Bull's-eye, peppermint, a piece of licorice—all lumped together in his cheek. For the moment, the park was forgotten.

He watched the girl advance without interest.

'Mama says you must come 'n eat.' She stared at his bulging cheek, one hand rubbing the side of her nose. 'Gimme.' He gave her a bull's-eye which she dropped into her mouth between dabs at her nose.

'Wipe your snot!' he ordered her, showing his

superiority. He walked past. She followed, sucking and sniffing.

When they entered the kitchen their father was
already seated at the table.

'Why must I always send somebody after you?'
his mother said.

He slipped into his seat and then hurriedly got
up to wash his hands before his mother could find
fault with yet another point.

Supper was a silent affair except for the scraping of spoon across plate and an occasional sniff
from his sister.

Almost at the end of the meal a thought came
to mind. He sat, spoon poised in the air, shaken
by its magnitude. Why not go to the park after
dark? After it had closed its gates on the old men,
the children, the nurses with their prams. There
would be no one to stop him. He couldn't think
further. He was light-headed with the thought of
it. His mother's voice, as she related her day to
his father, was not the steam which stung but a
soft breeze wafting past him, leaving him undis-
turbed. Qualms troubled him. He had never been
in that part of town at night. A band of fear
tightened across his chest, contracting his insides,
making it hard for him to swallow his food. He
gripped his spoon more tightly, stretching the skin
across his knuckles.

I'll do it! I'll go to the park as soon as we're
finished eating. He controlled himself with difficulty. He swallowed what was left on his plate
and furtively checked to see how the others were
faring. Hurry it up! Hurry it up!

When his father pushed the last plate aside and
lit a cigarette, he hastily cleared the table and began washing up.

Each piece of crockery washed, he passed on to his sister whose sniffing kept pace with their combined operation.

The dishes done, he swept the kitchen and carried out the garbage bin.

'Can I go out and play, mama?'

'Don't let me have to send for you again.'

His father remained silent, buried behind his newspaper.

'Before you go,' his mother stopped him, 'light the lamp and hang it in the passage.'

He filled the lamp with paraffin, turned up its wick and lit it. The light glimmered weakly through the streaked glass.

The moon to him was a fluorescent ball—light without warmth—and the stars, fragments chipped off it. Beneath street lights card games were in session. As he walked past, he sniffed the nostril-prickling smell of dagga. Dim doorways could not conceal couples clutching at each other.

Once clear of the district he broke into a jog-trot. He did not slacken his pace as he passed through downtown with its wonderland shop windows. As he neared the park his elation seeped out and his footsteps dragged.

In front of him was the park with its gate and iron railings. Behind the railings stood impaled the notice board. He could see the swings beyond. The sight strengthened him.

He walked over, his breath coming faster. There was no one in sight. A car turned the corner and came towards him and he started at the sound of its engine. The car swept past, the tyres softly licking the asphalt.

The railings were icy-cold to his touch and the shock sent him into action. He extended his arms and with monkey-like movements pulled himself up to perch on top of the railings, then dropped on the newly-turned earth.

The grass was damp with dew and he swept his feet across it. Then he ran and the wet grass bowed beneath his bare feet.

He ran from the swings to the merry-go-round, see-saw to chute, hands covering the metal.

Up the steps to the top of the chute. He stood outlined against the sky. He was a bird, an eagle. He flung himself down on his stomach, sliding swiftly. Wheeeeeeeeh! He rolled over when he slammed on to the grass. He was looking at the moon for an instant, then propelled himself to his feet and ran for the steps of the chute to recapture that feeling of flight. Each time he swept down the chute he wanted the trip never to end, to go on sliding, sliding, sliding.

He walked reluctantly past the see-saw, consoling himself with pushing at one end to send it wacking on the grass.

'Damn it!' he grunted as he strained to set the merry-go-round in motion. Thigh tensed, leg stretched, he pushed. The merry-go-round moved. He increased his exertion and jumped on, one leg trailing at the ready, to shove if it should slow down. The merry-go-round dipped and swayed. To keep it moving, he had to push more than he rode. Not wanting to spoil his pleasure he jumped off and raced for the swings.

Feet astride, hands clutching silver chains, he jerked his body to gain momentum. He crouched like a runner, then violently straightened. The swing widened its arc. It swept higher, higher, higher. It reached the sky. He could touch the moon. He plucked a star to pin to his breast. The earth was far below him. No bird could fly as high as he. Upwards and onwards he went.

A light switched on in the hut at the far side of the park. It was a small patch of yellow on a dark square. The door opened and he saw a dark figure in the doorway, then the door was shut and the figure strode towards him. He knew it was the attendant. A torch glinted brightly in the moonlight, as it swung at his side.

He continued swinging.

The attendant came to a halt in front of him, out of reach of the swing's arc, and flashed his torch. The light caught him in mid-air.

'God-dammit!' the attendant swore, 'I've told you before you can't get on the swings.'

The rattle of chains when the boy shifted his feet was the only answer he received.

'Why did you come back?'

'The swings. I came back for the swings.'

The attendant catalogued the things denied them because of their colour. Even his job depended on their goodwill.

'Blerry whites! They got everything.'

All his feelings urged him to leave the boy alone, to let him continue to enjoy himself. But the fear that someone might see them hardened him.

'Get off! Go home!' he screamed, his voice harsh, his anger directed at the system that drove him against his own. 'If you don't get off, I'll go for the police. You know what they'll do to you.'

The swing raced back and forth.

The attendant turned and raced towards the gate.

'Mama. Mama.' His lips trembled, wishing himself safe in his mother's kitchen sitting next to the still-burning stove with a comic spread across his knees. 'Mama. Mama.' His voice mounted, wrenching from his throat, keeping pace with the soaring swing as it climbed to the sky. Voice and swing. Swing and voice. Higher. Higher. Higher. Until they were one.

At the entrance to the park the notice board stood tall, its shadow elongated, pointing towards him.

The Living and the Dead
Ezekiel Mphahlele

. . ."It's all Jackson's fault," Stoffel said. "He goes out yesterday and instead of being here in the evening to prepare supper he doesn't come. This morning he's still not here, still not here, and I can't get my bloody breakfast in time because I've to do it myself, and you know *I must* have a good breakfast every day. Worse, my clock is out of order, buggered up, man, and the bloody Jackson's not here to wake me up. So I oversleep —that's what happens—and after last night's *braaivleis,* you know. It's five o'clock on a Friday morning, and the bastard hasn't turned up yet.' . . .

He liked Jackson, his cook, who had served him with the devotion of a trained animal and ministered to all his bachelor whims and eating habits for four years. . . .

From *In Corner B,* by Ezekiel Mphahlele. Reprinted by permission of East African Publishing House, Ltd.

Jackson had taken his usual Thursday off. He had gone to Shanty-Town, where his mother-in-law lived with his two children, in order to fetch them and take them to the zoo. He had promised so many times to take them there. His wife worked in another suburb. She couldn't go with them to the zoo because, she said, she had the children's sewing to finish. . . .

Stoffel's mind turned around in circles without ever coming to a fixed point. . . . His head was ringing with the voices he had heard so many times at recent meetings. Angry voices of residents who were gradually being incensed by speakers like him, frantic voices that demanded that the number of servants in each household be brought down because it wouldn't do for blacks to run the suburbs from their quarters in European backyards.

But there were also angry voices from other meetings: if you take the servants away, how are they going to travel daily to be at work on time, before we leave for work ourselves? Other voices: who told you there are too many natives in our yards? Then others: we want to keep as many servants as we can afford. . . .

Some of these kaffir lovers, of course, hate the thought of having to forego the fat feudal comfort of having cheap labour within easy reach when we remove black servants to their own locations, Stoffel mused.

And amid these voices he saw himself working and sweating to create a theory to defend ready-made attitudes, stock attitudes that various people had each in their own time planted in him: his mother, his father, his brothers, his friends, his schoolmasters, his university professors and all

the others who claimed him as their own. He was
fully conscious of the whole process in his mind.
Things had to be done with conviction or not at
all. . . .

He surrendered himself to it all, to this violent
desire to remain part of a brutal historic past, lest
he should be crushed by the brutal necessities of
the present, he should be forced to lose his identity: Almighty God, no, no! . . .

When he woke from a stupor, Stoffel Visser remembered Jackson's wife over at Greenside. He
had not asked her if she knew where his servant
was. He jumped up and dialled on his telephone.
He called Virginia's employer and asked him. No,
Virginia didn't know where her husband was. As
far as she knew her husband had told her the
previous Sunday that he was going to take the
children to the zoo. What could have happened to
her husband, she wanted to know. Why hadn't he
telephoned the police? Why hadn't he phoned
Virginia in the morning? Virginia's master asked
him these and several other questions. He got annoyed because he couldn't answer them.

* * *

None of the suburban police stations or Mar-
shall Square Station had Jackson's name in their
charge books. They would let him know "if anything turned up." A young voice from one police
station said perhaps Stoffel's "kaffir" had gone to
sleep with his "maid" elsewhere and had forgotten
to turn up for work. Or, he suggested, Jackson
might be under a hang-over in the location. "You
know what these kaffirs are." And he laughed
with a thin sickly voice. Stoffel banged the receiver down.

There was a light knock at the door of his flat. . . .

Jackson's wife, Virginia. . . .

"He's not yet here, Master?"

"No." Impulsively he showed her to a chair in the kitchen. "Where else could he have gone?"

"Don't know, Master." Then she started to cry, softly. "Sunday we were together, Master, at my master's place. We talked about our children and you know one is seven the other four and few months and firstborn is just like his father with eyes and nose and they have always been told about the zoo by playmates so they wanted to go there, so Jackson promised them he would take them to see the animals." She paused, sobbing quietly, as if she meant that to be the only way she could punctuate her speech.

"And the smaller child loves his father so and he's Jackson's favourite. You know Nkati the elder one was saying to his father the other day the day their grandmother brought them to see us —he says I wish you die, just because his father wouldn't give him more sweets, Lord he's going to be the rebel of the family and he needs a strong man's hand to keep him straight. And now if Jackson is—is—oh Lord God above."

She sobbed freely now.

"All right. I'll try my best to find him, wherever he may be. You may go now, because it's time for me to lock up."

"Thank you, Master." She left. . . .

* * *

Monday lunch-time Stoffel Visser motored to his flat, just to check up. He found Jackson in his room lying on his bed. His servant's face was all swollen up with clean bandages covering the whole head and cheeks. His eyes sparkled from the surrounding puffed flesh.

"Jackson!"

His servant looked up at him.

"What happened?"

"The police."

"Where?"

"Victoria Police Station."

"Why?"

"They call me monkey."

"Who?"

"White man in train."

"Tell me everything, Jackson." Stoffel felt his servant was resisting him. He read bitterness in the stoop of Jackson's shoulders and in the whole profile as he sat up.

"You think I'm telling lie, Master? Black man always tell lie, eh?"

"No, Jackson. I can only help if you tell me everything." Somehow the white man managed to keep his patience.

"I take children to zoo. Coming back I am reading my night-school book. White man come into train and search everyone. One see me reading and say what's this monkey think he's doing with a book. He tell me stand up, he shouts like it's first time for him to talk to a human being. That's what baboons do when they see man. I am hot and boiling and I catch him by his collar and tie and shake him. Ever see a *marula* tree that's heavy with fruit? That's how I shake him. Other white men take me to place in front, a small room. Everyone there hits me hard. At station they push me out on platform and I fall on one knee. They lift me up and take me to police station. Not in

city but far away I don't know where but I see
now it must have been Victoria Station. There
they charge me with drunken noise. Have you a
pound? I say no and I ask them they must ring
you, they say if I'm cheeky they will hell me up
and then they hit and kick me again. They let me
go and I walk many miles to hospital. I'm in
pain." Jackson paused, bowing his head lower.

When he raised it again he said, "I lose letter
from my father with my beautiful pictures."

Stoffel sensed agony in every syllable, in every
gesture of the hand. He had read the same story
so many times in newspapers and had never given
it much thought.

He told Jackson to lie in bed, and for the first
time in four years he called a doctor to examine
and treat his servant. He had always sent him or
taken him to hospital.

For four years he had lived with a servant and
had never known more about him than that he had
two children living with his mother-in-law and a
wife. Even then they were such distant abstrac-
tions—just names representing some persons, not
human flesh and blood and heart and mind.

And anger came up in him to muffle the cry of
shame, to shut out the memory of recent events
that was battering on the iron bars he had built up
in himself as a means of protection. There were
things he would rather not think about. And the
heat of his anger crowded them out. What next?
He didn't know. Time, time, time, that's what he
needed to clear the whole muddle beneath the fog
that rose thicker and thicker with the clash of
currents from the past and the present. Time,
time . . .

And then Stoffel Visser realised he did not want

to think, to feel. He wanted to do something . . .
Jackson would want a day off to go to his father
. . . Sack Jackson? No. Better continue treating
him as a name, not as another human being. Let
Jackson continue as a machine to work for him.
Meantime, he must do his duty—dispatch the
commission's report. That was definite, if nothing
else was. He was a white man, and he must be responsible. To be white and to be responsible were
one and the same thing . . .

religion

For thousands of years religion has been a vital
social institution in Africa. African writers often
describe traditional religious life and show how it
provided solidarity and meaning for its people. In
Camara Laye's autobiography, The African Child,
which is set in Guinea, the father is an important
religious figure. As head of the goldsmiths, an il-
lustrious occupation in traditional Guinea, he is
in communication with the Spirit of the community. Normally he would proudly pass on this special gift to his eldest son. He is telling his little
boy about this when he suddenly realizes that the
son will be away at school too much ever to re-
ceive the training necessary to succeed his father.
So far the father is aware only that his son will be
excluded. Later he may realize that the religion itself will fall apart, as happens in another novel,
Arrow of God, by Chinua Achebe. Some African
writers dwell on the deaths of the traditional gods.
Others are impressed by the renaissance of traditional African religion.

Christianity has been in Africa a long time. In

*Ethiopia the Coptic church has been in existence
2000 years. In the Congo, West and South Africa,
from the fifteenth century on, Christian chaplains
often accompanied European explorers on their
voyages around the continent and for years at a
time lived with them in castle forts. Often they
started schools to which they invited the sons of
African political leaders. Christian missions became highly organized and expanded during the
nineteenth century. To Ghana and Nigeria came
black Sierra Leoneans, Caribbeans and black Ca-
nadians along with white colleagues.*

*Hundreds of churches and schools had been
established by the 1880s when Afram, hero of*
The Catechist, *became an orphaned schoolboy
working as a servant in his schoolmaster's home
to pay tuition, board and room.*

*In the West a lore has grown up about the
preacher and his family. Abruquah in* The Catechist *adds to the lore about the African pastor and
his family. A catechist in Ghana is more like a
supply pastor in North America. He is a full-time
church worker, but he lacks sufficient education
to be ordained. This work reads like a journal or
diary of memories. A "frontier psychology" affected Christians in West Africa much like the
frontier situations that confronted North American clergymen in the nineteenth century. In any
case, whether preacher in America or catechist in
Ghana, in both places there are the frequent
moves from town to town, the indignation over
church politics and the frustration of trying to ed-
ucate the children in rural or "bush" schools. In
both places there is the appreciaiton of the wife:
"She was a find," Afram says about his wife. In
both places there is the humble realization of the*

husband: "Those who worked for the Lord were in the greatest peril concerning their salvation."

In his autobiography, Down Second Avenue, Mphahlele deals with his very close connection with various churches, clergymen and mission schools—and their direct confrontation with the racist institutions of South Africa. Blaxall is a white Anglican missionary who in recent years suffered under "house arrest" imposed by the South African government. Father Wardell was Mphahlele's white parish rector at one time.

Mphahlele sees the paradox of Christian men caught in the operations of the institutional racism of the church. He sees the irony in the fact that many white South Africans assume that it is the blacks in that country who fall into the category of savagery and barbarism (using nineteenth century anthropological terms), when in reality it is the whites who are barbaric and in great need of the Christian mission. Mphahlele sees the ambiguity of "civilization": white South Africans enjoy an industrial, technological, affluent society, but have systematically set out to destroy the personhood of millions of blacks and other nonwhites. Black South Africans suffer without conveniences and comforts, but yearn for a society that fulfils personhood in freedom. Who is civilized?

Rabearivelo was born in Malagasy. He was writing poetry at the turn of the century. Recently his poetry has been translated from the French. In this poem he shows his awareness of the vitality of Islam and Christianity and their long history on the African continent.

In Ngugi's A Grain of Wheat, *Gikonyo has returned from Kenyan concentration camps to find his wife, Mumbi, with a child fathered by the man who betrayed him to the white settlers. Gikonyo refuses to ask Mumbi how it happened. He also refuses to acknowledge the existence of the child. Mumbi tries in many ways to bring up the subject, but Gikonyo refuses until the moment when this selection opens.*

What are the promises of all religion? The African Child seeks cultural wholeness. The Catechist asks one last thing: acceptance. Mphahlele wants freedom and social justice. Mumbi and Gikonyo ask for reconciliation. In Rabearivelo's poem, he prays for oneness. Herein lies mission: the meeting of these promises with faith.

The African Child
Camara Laye

"You can see for yourself that I am not more gifted than any other man, that I have nothing which other men have not also, and even that I have less than others, since I give everything away, and would even give away the last thing I had, the shirt on my back. Nevertheless, I am better known than other men, and my name is on everyone's tongue, and it is I who have authority over all the blacksmiths in the five cantons. If these things are so, it is by virtue of this snake alone, who is the guiding spirit of our race. It is

From *The African Child*, © Camara Laye, 1954. Reprinted by permission of Collins Publishers, London and Farrar, Straus & Giroux, Inc., New York.

to this snake that I owe everything, and it is he
likewise who gives me warning of all that is to
happen. Thus I am never surprised, when I
awake, to see this or that person waiting for me
outside my workshop: I already know that he or
she will be there. No more am I surprised when
this or that motor bicycle or bicycle breaks down,
or when an accident happens to a clock: because
I had foreknowledge of what would come to pass.
Everything is transmitted to me in the course of
the night, together with an account of all the work
I shall have to perform, so that from the start,
without having to cast about in my mind, I know
how to repair whatever is brought to me; and it is
these things that have established my renown as a
craftsman. But all this—let it never be forgotten
—I owe to the snake, I owe it to the guiding spirit
of our race."

He was silent; and then I understood why,
when my father used to come back from a walk he
could enter the workshop and say to the appren-
tices: "During my absence, this or that person has
been here, he was dressed in such and such a way,
he came from such and such a place and he
brought with him such and such a piece of work
to be done." And all marvelled at this curious
knowledge. Now I understood how my father ob-
tained his information. When I raised my eyes, I
saw that my father was watching me.

"I have told you all these things, little one, because you are my son, the eldest of my sons, and
because I have nothing to hide from you. There is
a certain form of behaviour to observe, and certain ways of acting in order that the guiding spirit
of our race may approach you also. I, your father,
was observing that form of behaviour which per-
suades our guiding spirit to visit us. Oh, perhaps

not consciously. But nevertheless it is true that if you desire the guiding spirit of our race to visit you one day, if you desire to inherit it in your turn, you will have to conduct yourself in the selfsame manner; from now on, it will be necessary for you to be more and more in my company."

He gazed at me with burning eyes, then suddenly he heaved a sigh.

"I fear, I very much fear, little one, that you are not often enough in my company. You are all day at school, and one day you shall depart from that school for a greater one. You will leave me, little one. . . ."

And again he heaved a sigh. I saw that his heart was heavy within him. The hurricane-lamp hanging on the veranda cast a harsh glare on his face. He suddenly seemed to me like an old man.

"Father!" I cried.

"Son . . ." he whispered.

And I was no longer sure whether I ought to continue to attend the school or whether I ought to remain in the workshop; I felt unutterably confused.

The Catechist
Joseph W. Abruquah

When I started work as a catechist at the Abura Dunkwa Infant-junior school, I was the evangelist and headmaster and only teacher. I was a brilliant

From *The Catechist,* © George Allen and Unwin, Ltd., 1965. Reprinted by permission of the author.

scholar, it is true, but my standard was still abominably low compared with the standards of today. I did not know this then, and I did the best I could about drumming the Roman alphabet and multiplication tables into the heads of thirty noisy kids whom I soon reduced to some semblance of discipline with the aid of a little twig which did the work of a cane.

On Sundays I conducted service in a little Wesleyan Chapel and preached to a congregation just emerging from paganism, myself a near pagan. I don't think Christianity meant more to those people or to me than a mere substitute for the witchdoctor. . . .

I was preparing to enter the Ministry all the time, and never for one moment did I imagine that I should stop where I was—a teacher-catechist. Certain incidents helped to incite me to great hopes and yet helped to thwart my progress.

One such incident occurred when a European missionary stopped one day at my station. The shock of surprise with which he regarded me and expressed disgust that I should be put in a place of that type tickled my vanity.

'Who brought you here, Mr. Afram?' he asked. 'You should enter the Ministry at once and not rot in a place like this. I am going to write a strong letter to the Chairman about you, and to your superintendent Minister.'

I did my best to say that I had asked to be stationed there so that I could make ends meet with my increased salary of £1 10s. and what my wife could bring in. But he sent the telegram to my superintendent Minister at Cape Coast:—

'Remove Afram from Abura Dunkwa at once.

He is not a man to be put in a place of that type. Send him at once to be trained as a Minister.'

Somehow I think that sealed my doom, for human jealousy and malice seem to breed in the very midst of the institution whose work it is to rid the world of them; I was in disfavour from then on. But the life of a Catechist is an exciting one, and my wife was a find. She made everything so deceptively light for me that I never thought of finding an alternative source of employment till much later, too late in life. . . .

It was after [the] first child was born that I thought I should try getting into the Ministry under my own steam, and I took the necessary tests. I am convinced I came up top in the scripture examination, but I failed to get into the Ministry. . . .

My failure . . . at first left me undaunted, for I was still a young man with plenty of life ahead of me: I would get in in time.

* * *

The spirit of the Lord was upon me as I changed station after station south of the Pra river, but my crowning glory was when I was transferred to Ashanti, the citadel of paganism at the time. . . .

* * *

With six very healthy children in the house I had my work cut out. Trying to cope with their problems, I found my Christian principles sadly inadequate. I tolerated their sins until I could stand it no longer; then I beat them and they stoned me or were rude to me. . . .

I am afraid I did not give the problems at home much serious thought—I never consciously tried to be Christian at home. I just gave natural impulses free play, and I certainly did a lot of harm I did not know of at the time.

But my little Christian flock outside in the village increased with my triumph over witchcraft. . . .

* * *

Imagine my consternation when I received a telegram asking me to prepare to move to Yeji: —'Afram get ready to proceed to Yeji' is a message I shall remember to my dying day. For I failed my Mission and the church, I failed my God, and I failed myself. Because I failed, the church did not advance its frontiers farther north than Ashanti!

* * *

I could not go to Yeji. I had not the courage to risk going so near to the Northern Territories. The only thing I knew about the North was the warlike fearlessness of the tribes who were still untouched by Pax Britannica. . . .

It was too dangerous to risk the safety of my family. The Church had persisted in refusing to encourage my advancement from the wretched condition of a village Catechist, but when it came to doing the dirty work they were ready to sacrifice me without any qualms. I refused to proceed to Yeji, and waited for the repercussions.

The Superintendent Minister of Kumasi was sent down to convince me. I succeeded in convincing him that it was a job for a bachelor, not a family man.

'Look at my children! You don't expect me to go tramping north to Yeji, do you?'

'Remember the early Missionaries, Afram. They went where the Spirit ordered them to.'

'Yes, Sir, but the Spirit says I should not go.'

'What Spirit? Surely the selfish reasons you have given now do not stand for the Spirit I am talking about? You should not try to blaspheme. God has ordered you to Yeji—'

'You mean you have ordered me!—Who is blaspheming this time?'

'But it is God's work.'

'How would you like to go yourself, if you were in my place?'

'If I were in your place, I would pray to God to give me strength to do His will. Brother Afram, let us pray.'

We prayed. I was even more convinced after the prayer that it was a bachelor's work. . . .

* * *

The immediate effect of my great refusal was to be transferred nearer my home town to a village in Agona circuit where, again, I helped in the village school. . . .

The work of the church went on with my former zeal. I read the Bible every morning, prepared my sermons, visited my congregation in their homes, and buried the dead. Only a few months after my arrival there was a notable change in the financial position of the church. They had enough money to think of building a new school—a proper school for their children. I organised harvests, special collections and a fund for the new buildings for which a site had been acquired.

I was beginning to be quite happy, when a new Minister came to the circuit. He was stationed at Nyakrom but paid his usual visits to my station. The Rev. Ako was a tall, fat, rather pot-bellied Minister who tended to show off—and I hated any showing off. He insisted on calling me 'Catechist,' which infuriated me. I believe the psychologists would say I had developed a 'complex,' but whatever it was, I never wanted to identify myself with any stupid group. I was a class apart—it was only sheer bad luck which had made me stagnate in this profession . . . he had no call to degrade me in front of my congregation by emphasising the gulf which lay between Ministers and Catechists. But when his authority trespassed on my private home management, that was the limit. I was furious and nearly came to blows with the man. . . .

Amongst of the joyful occurrences at Nsaba was the building of the school which I started but did not complete. The school-children did most of the work of carrying the sand, mixing the cement and carrying the cement blocks when completed to the workmen. . . .

I loved the place and never thought I was to leave it so suddenly. But leave I must owing to the quarrel with the Minister. There was no need to transfer me; for I was working wonderfully well with the congregation. My 'Harvest' fetched in almost as much money as the central town, and I encouraged the school to stage concerts . . . and I got more money for the church.

I am inclined to think that, like most workers in the Methodist Church, I paid too much attention to this side of my work. It was always 'money, money, money,' and I was good at drawing it out of people. I did not spare myself in this direction, although I now think very few souls are saved this way. The women were wonderful. They paid their class and ticket money at all costs and I saw that they were buried with their latest ticket in their right hand. . . .

A week after my quarrel with the Rev. Ako I received a telegram telling me of my transfer to Bobikuma in the same circuit—a much poorer station. . . .

To think that I collected as much as £30 at one harvest, gave the most accurate account of it, and was given £3 per quarter is enough to turn a saint into the devil himself. . . .

Always on the move. I was only a few months at Bobikuma; a year at the next Station, and so on until I was transferred farther and farther from home again. At most stations I replaced in-efficient Ministers who had ruined the mission house, estranged their congregations and neg-lected their duty in various little ways. I sweated to put matters on a sounder basis all round, but the end was always the same. They raised an out-cry! What had they done to deserve a Catechist? 'Remember our former glory. This is one of the oldest churches in the country. We want a Min-ister.' And rightly so. But that sort of thing tends to lead one to think it a curse to become such I was. . . .

I was transferred to one of the oldest missions in the country, where I was to do the active work of the circuit under an invalid Minister.

It was a worthwhile job, and I enjoyed most of it because the Minister understood me and we had little cause for friction. There was also a school for the children and in them I found quite

a lot to live for. They would one day honour me
and shame my enemies if I saw to their education; so I saw to it. . . .

* * *

'Papa, Papa! Mammie! Simeon is here!' . . .

A tall strapping lad of about sixteen came
bursting into the hall just at that moment and I
beheld my own son Simeon. . . . The main
thing was that he brought very good news. He had
finished the elementary school and had got
through his entrance examination at Wesley College.

After that we surrendered ourselves to general
merriment. There was laughter galore, such as
we in Africa know so well. . . .

'Papa, I am glad to be home,' he said. 'This
Wesley College, is it going to be too expensive?
I mean, there are no fees, but the clothes and
transport.'

'Oh, don't worry. I must see you through this.
It is my life. You are going to Wesley College, so
don't you worry your little head.'

Very soon afterwards . . . he was off again.
His big trunk, which happened to be the trunk I
gave to his mother before her marriage, was filled
with white drill suits, brand new shoes and other
articles of clothing: Each suit cost about 8s. to
make. The shoes were 6s. 1d. a pair from Len-
nards. I was receiving only £3 per month, £9 a
quarter, as pay.

* * *

The year was 1928. Place: a few miles from
Cape Coast. We had lorries, both Chevrolets, one
carrying my personal effects—luggage, furniture,

etc., the other carrying more personal effects and
the family. . . .

When was it going to stop, this wandering? This
was the constant preoccupation of many who
found themselves in a similar plight. It wasn't only
Catechists, it hit all civil servants, Ministers,
teachers, etc.

'The Foxes have holes and the birds of the air
have nests, but the son of man . . .'

That is how I left Anomabu in 1928 to travel
140 miles to Appollonia or Nzima as the inhabit-
ants preferred it to be called . . . to me it meant
retracing all these miles at some future date. If,
for instance, my wife died or some relative died,
I would have had to go home or cut myself off
from family obligations. In fact, as I repeated
afterwards a thousand times, I was lost to the
world. Meanwhile: 'Is that you, Mr. Afram?'
asked the Minister in charge of the circuit. . . .
'I am putting you at Atuabu because I feel you
are the most competent man for such an important outpost.' . . .

* * *

The house would be quiet for some hours, while
the women reeked of cooking smoke. I would
relax in my favourite chair and read aloud a
treatise on St. Paul in readiness for a last bid for
the Ministry. I didn't understand much of it, but
I have met full-fledged parsons who were no better. I would doze off. . . .

* * *

It seemed that the Reverend Minister was not
satisfied with my circuit accounts. He could not
understand how I could maintain a son at a train-

ing college, rear seven other children, feed them
and send them all to school, on a salary barely
sufficient to feed one man. It seems I was foolish
in serving him with food he was not used to eating at home and which he must have thought was
our usual daily fare. . . .

I must confess I have little tact when aroused
by such traitorous acts of suspicion. . . . I must
have looked like thunder. . . . 'Scrutinize' my
accounts, as if I was a common felon! In my anger
I had the support of all my flock. The circuit
steward who really kept all the money was even
more annoyed than I was.

The 'scrutiny' took place at a full meeting of
local Catechists, Leaders and the Minister. Every
item was correct, of course. I would rather go on
short commons than embezzle church funds.

'Afram,' said the Minister, afterwards, 'You are
a wonderful man!' . . .

[I moved to Anomabu] . . . I spared no efforts to put the financial position of my church on
a sounder basis. I preached with spirit and fervour and soaked my tattered shirts in perspira-
tion for the souls of my congregation. I sweated
even more to collect dues and the class-and-
ticket money at which I had won quite a reputa-
tion. When the circuit steward saw my zeal, he
joined me whole-heartedly in a Sunday-by-Sunday
exhortation.

'Anomabu Church is a disgrace,' he said. 'This
was the Ebenezer Church founded by Thomas
Birch Freeman, one of the first churches in the
Gold Coast and as old as the church at Cape
Coast. We have always had a proper Minister
here. If you want a Minister, then you must pay
your dues. It is not fitting that this Church should
be led by a Catechist. It is disgraceful.' . . .

When he had finished I wished I could sink beneath the ground. My congregation dared not look at me in my disgrace . . . What a soul-searing experience! I had to bear this on Sunday after Sunday for years . . . on occasions when some thanksgiving service brought strangers in their hundreds to Anomabu's Ebenezer Chapel, it was the resuscitated supernumerary Minister who kept the church from exposure. He was their Minister! No wonder it became an obsession with me that one of my sons, at least, must be a Minister. . . .

But my days at Anomabu were numbered. I was too old; I had nearly died on their hands: I must be transferred to a smaller station. . . .

'Mr. Afram, you must retire! You are too old. Your sons will look after you!' said the Minister.

'Has Ekuban retired? Ministers like him are older than I am and have sons to look after them,' I thought.

But they knew the work of the Catechist was a very different kettle of fish. To them I was too old! Too old? I would show them. I carried on. In 1944 I was transferred to Asamankese to put another church right. . . .

But the best news was that Simeon was accepted for training for the Ministry! The sum of all my hopes had added up. At last my disgrace was wiped clean by my children. . . . Simeon was training to be a MINISTER. If his father had not made it, he had. . . .

The Lord be praised! . . .

* * *

1948 was a year of achievement for me and mine. My son had become a Minister. Another son became a B.A. . . .

In setting down my experiences as a parent and

Catechist, I have sought to hide very little of my
shortcomings and those of my children. It is my
firm belief that workers in the Lord's vineyard
are in greater peril of their souls than most of the
people they seek to save. I have shown my begin-
nings and the foundation of African superstition
upon which my Christian beliefs were laid. I have
also revealed the poverty of my education and
the burning desire to do better by my children. I
have already shown the path that service took me
through my youthful pioneering days in the villages of Ashanti and the constant threat to my
life from disease and witchcraft, and I have shown
how I disobeyed the call to duty in favour of my
wife and children. . . .

My religious beliefs have been of the simplest.
I have been unable to live up to most of Christ's
teaching, but have still a firm belief in God and
his power to save me from myself. Now that I
can look back on my life, I can see where maybe
I failed. But in the thick of life's struggle events
have led me on and I had no time to analyse my
reactions to them. I believe that with the rest of
the world I took my punishment in full, in blood
and toil and tribulations manifold.

* * *

. . . Kwesi arrived from England. . . . I wish
I had had more to offer him than that ramshackle
hut and the bare room with its aged bed. This was
no place to come to after the luxury of England,
but there was nowhere else I could call my
home. . . .

My prestige, which had fallen to rock bottom,
began to rise again. . . . My son was indeed a
graduate, far more learned than anyone I knew,

and a European in many things. . . . The Lord
had not altogether forsaken me and mine. . . .

I had worked half a century to bring salvation
to other people. It would probably be appropriate
to say, 'Physician heal thyself.' . . .

At the throne of God, I hope the Almighty will
not deal too harshly with his servant, but in His
infinite mercy will forgive my sins and accept
even me.

Down Second Avenue
Ezekiel Mphahlele

Towards the end of 1940, someone from a
Reef town wrote to the principal of Adams College asking if he could recommend a student due
to leave college who might want to work in an
institution for the blind as a clerk. The head
master of the teacher-training department put
the proposition to me. I was intrigued by it. I
don't know what it was that attracted me towards
the work, because I had always passionately
wanted to be a teacher. . . .

So in a moment of reckless abandon I went to
'Ezenzeleni,' the only institution for the care of
African blind in the area covered by the Trans-
vaal, the Orange Free State and Natal. The man
who had written to Adams was the Rev. Arthur
William Blaxall (now Doctor), then superin-

From *Down Second Avenue,* © Ezekiel Mphahlele,
1959. Reprinted by permission of Faber and Faber, Ltd.
and Curtis Brown, Ltd.

tendent and secretary. I remember vividly now the
afternoon he fetched me by van from Roodepoort
station, twelve miles out of Johannesburg, in January of 1941. I was twenty-two, a great deal confused, utterly unsure of myself, but feeling a kind
of inevitability as I entered the service of Ezenzeleni.

I was given an hour a day to teach myself touch
typing from a manual. . . . After learning driving from Mr. Blaxall over about two months, I
delivered blind-made goods in suburban Johannesburg and near-by towns. I carried baskets, mat-
tresses—some clean and some smelling of ancient
urine—in and out of the van. I collected mail in
the mornings by van. Twice a week I taught a few
literate blind men how to type, a job I enjoyed
immensely. I was paid £6 10s. a month—what
I would be earning if I were a full-time teacher.
. . . One Sunday in the month I took the blind
men and women to church in the location about
half a mile away. I continued to attend the Anglican church in the location and morning Mass in
the institution chapel, which Mr. Blaxall conducted. Again with a sense of inevitability. . . .

* * *

One evening Father Wardle, C. R., then in
charge of Holy Cross Anglican Church in Or-
lando, visited me.

'It's about your church shillings,' Father Wardle said, after we nibbled at topics of general conversation. 'Between you and your wife there is
£2 7s. owing. I know things are difficult for you
these days, but I just thought I should remind
you. Another thing is your attendance at church.

Do you find it difficult to reconcile your religion
with your politics?'

'Extremely so,' I said.

'Have you tried praying about it?'

'Yes. I've given up trying to pray—formally I
mean. I just think and think and think.'

'It's hard for everybody.'

'Not for the white man.' He dropped his head
and toyed with the crucifix suspended on his belt,
and the pathos on his face annoyed me a little.

Father Wardle couldn't have come at a worse
moment about these things. About the same week
a young man I used to teach at the high school
had come to seek advice about a case he had
against the African police at the local station.
They had met him in the township and demanded
his pass. When he produced it they said it was not
genuine, and arrested him. At the station they
had caught hold of him and stretched him on a
bench while a white constable beat him with a
leather belt on bare buttocks. They had then released him. He showed me the weals and I took
him to a medical doctor for a certificate. We had
laid a charge at the same police-station, and the
young man had identified the policeman who beat
him.

Every time the case came on, it was reported
that the constable couldn't attend. I wrote to the
District Commandant of Police about this and
we had to give it up eventually.

The young man's case recalled to mind, then,
that of Rebecca [my wife] who had been assaulted
six months before by a white ticket examiner in
a train. There was an argument about a ticket,
and the white man had used abusive language and

pulled her out of the train at a station with such
force that Rebecca had sprained her ankle. She
had laid a charge but the man had never appeared
in court. Every time he was reported ill. She had
then paid a lawyer £15 to take up a civil case
against the man. A year after the incident the
man, still in the railways, was forced to attend as
it was a civil case. He was found guilty and ordered to pay Rebecca £10 damages! That was
much later, after our interview with Father Wardle. Rebecca had just had another postponement
of the case when the young man came. Yes, Father Wardle couldn't have come at a worse time.

'Just now, I don't think it's fair for anybody to
tell me to expect a change of heart among a
bunch of madmen who are determined not to cede
an inch, or to listen to reason. It is unfair to ask
me to subsist on mission-school sermons about
Christian conduct and passive resistance in circumstances where it is considered a crime to be
decent; where a policeman will run me out of my
house at the point of a sten gun when I try to
withhold my labour. For years I have been told
by white and Black preachers to love my neighbour; love him when there's a bunch of whites
who reckon they are Israelites come out of Egypt
in obedience to God's order to come and civilize
heathens; a bunch of whites who feed on the sym-
bolism of God's race venturing into the desert
among the ungodly. For years now I have been
thinking it was all right for me to feel spiritually
strong after a church service. And now I find it
is not the kind of strength that answers the demand of suffering humanity around me. It doesn't
even seem to answer the longings of my own
heart.'

The priest sat and listened. Again the pathos on his face annoyed me because I didn't know whether it reflected failure to understand the forces that were tearing inside me, or a feeling of pity.

'What *are* the longings of your heart?'

'What every man longs for which he begins to feel sharply when you whites make him feel insufficient.'

'You talk as if I represented the institution of white oppression,' he said.

'That's a tragedy the most decent of us are caught up in whether they like it or not.' I felt a devilish sort of pride in saying so, because that was one of the many times I have wished I could hate all whites: it would be so much simpler and less painful.

'You mustn't misjudge the missionaries, though, after all you were educated in mission schools and your children are in an Anglican nursery school. No government ever thought of building schools for you before the missionary came here, still less, nursery schools.'

'The age-old argument. Still you must admit that before Father Trevor Huddleston came on the scene—and that's only 1943—missionaries had let politics alone and consequently the forces of evil have had a start of about 300 years. During which time missionaries have abetted, connived at or stood aloof from, the white man's total disregard of justice and other human values. Even so, Trevor Huddleston was a lone fighter. The rest of the church in South Africa didn't speak his language.'

'Can I help you in this terrible conflict?'

'No one can help me. I intend to resolve it myself. There are more urgent matters than that. Like the buzzing and groaning and shrieking noises you hear in Shanty Town down there. A resolution of my personal conflicts could never alleviate the miseries of Shanty Town.'

I felt hollow, flat and I feared perhaps in my emotional outburst I had failed to make my point. Maybe I didn't really have a definite point. I told myself that I needed time to think, but really, I couldn't think. And my overcharged emotional response mechanism was my enemy. It has often been. All I knew was that my outlook on the Church had decidedly changed.

A few weeks later Father Wardle refused to baptize our third-born. Rebecca insisted on having him baptized. Little as I cared, I had decided not to stand in her way. But I knew that she was following a custom, and not a conviction, because we shared our disillusionment. From my own standpoint, I didn't feel competent to challenge her to it. Father Wardle's reasons for refusal were that if I didn't believe in the Church any more, and I owed money to the Church I had no right to its sacraments. But then I hadn't claimed any. Still, after a conscientious church councillor had urged him to change his mind, I had to be in our church that afternoon. I didn't even try to be mentally present. The service floated before me like the traffic in front of my house.

After that service I realized all the more how I hated formalism, especially when it contained an element of mysticism; how I detested formal allegiance to groups other than those closely connected with the arts and with the struggle to attain freedom. It had to be something I could *experience* within my then contracting pattern of sensory, emotional and mental responses. And I had outgrown the aesthetic experience of church worship. . . .

The last half of 1953 I worked for Arthur Blaxall as shorthand typist. He had retired from active blind welfare work, and was secretary of the Christian Council of South Africa. I was paid £20 per month, and he added £8 from his own pocket. . . .

I went to Basutoland in search of something. What it was I didn't know. But it was there, where it wasn't, inside me. Perhaps it was hate, maybe love, or both; or sordidness; maybe it was beauty. As I say, I didn't know. . . .

You get a feeling of static life in Moshoeshoe's country . . . the mountains seeming to approach and recede at the same time . . . the gorges left by the claws of Time . . . the Bushmen rock painting. . . .

My longing search continued. Mind and heart stood still. It tormented me to feel so insufficient, and not to know the why and wherefore. At times thought and feeling would gush forth in torrents so that many things became jumbled symbols of my hope and yearning. . . . But alas, my dreams had long since taken flight and now hung dry in shining cobwebs to which my fermenting furies clung crucified. . . .

Then an old man visited me. Arthur. We talked the night away, confiding in each other, learning from each other.

Dawn came and announced victory. The quest had come to an end, if the mere knowing of it seems to be the end.

I knew then what I had been looking for: a fatally beautiful lady called bitterness. . . . I've

tamed her. She's the mistress of my dull useless
moments; so I can stamp my foot on the ground
to have her once proud head chopped off—the
head that once launched a million corpuscles in
my blood which chafed against the roots of my
hair. But I may not just decide. Depends on the
other man. Tell it him. . . .

* * *

Arthur and Florence Blaxall have long left
Ezenzeleni. Arthur is organizing secretary of the
Christian Council of South Africa. To think of
them is to remember Ezenzeleni: Arthur walking
with a drooping shoulder because he lost a lung
in World War I. . . . Mrs. Blaxall . . . patiently going through the daily routine of teaching
the deaf, dumb and blind Radcliffe to express
himself, a boy she had adopted when he was moving on all fours as a result of spinal meningitis—
and trained to walk straight. . . .

. . . He was always probing young minds and
holding his ear to the ground to know other people's sufferings and seek a way to help. He has
always attended political and trade union meetings, learning patiently, but never condescending
or imposing himself. Now that my religious outlook has changed, I think of him as an enigma. It
continues to puzzle me how a man like him, un-
orthodox in his denominational allegiance and
missionary outlook, maintains steadfast Christian-
pacifist convictions in situations where the very
forces of oppression he does not like have thrown
all ethics to the winds. We disagree on many
points of political and religious practice, but the
picture that comes to my mind of him is always
that of the unmissionary missionary.

24 Poems
Jean-Joseph Rabearivelo

The worshipper ends her morning prayers
and comes to hear the children on the verandah
who recite aloud
their biblical lessons.
It sounds like a distant waterfall
leaping a moss grown rock
yonder, beyond the hills
where the Christians, surprised by the shadows
are reciting Muslim suras
beneath the pacific sky.

Looking through the leaves that fall
like a continuous flow of black tears,
I cannot distinguish anything
and hear only fragments of speech
in which words recur like Egypt
and Israel.

I step on a mound of earth
smelling the crushed and flattened grass
and I scatter the foliage that impedes my sight.
A small finch cries in the tree top
and I lift my eyes;
but what I see are the stars:
bulbous like garlick

From *24 Poems*, by Jean-Joseph Rabearivelo. Mbari
Publications, Ibadan, 1962.

spotted like quails
and they remind me of the prayers I have
   confused;
and it seems to me
that the flight from Pharao
took place in this azure desert of Imerina
here where all Religions meet—
and poems too.

A Grain of Wheat
James Ngugi

'I am going now,' she said. 'I may not come
tomorrow—or the next day.' She started to put
things in the bag determinedly. He wanted to say:
don't go. But he suddenly said: 'Let us talk about
the child.'

Mumbi, already on her feet, was surprised by
these words. She sat down again and looked at
him.

'In here, at the hospital?' she asked, without
any excitement.

'Now, yes.'

'No, not today,' she said, almost impatiently, as
if she was now really aware of her independence.
Gikonyo was surprised by the new firmness in her
voice.

'All right. When I leave the hospital,' he said,
and after an awkward pause, added: 'Will you go

From *A Grain of Wheat*, © James Ngugi, 1967. Reprinted by permission of Heinemann Educational Books,
Ltd.

back to the house, light the fire, and see things don't decay?'

She considered this for a while, her head turned aside. Then she looked at him, directly, in the eyes.

'No, Gikonyo. People try to rub out things, but they cannot. Things are not so easy. What has passed between us is too much to be passed over in a sentence. We need to talk, to open our hearts to one another, examine them, and then together plan the future we want. But now, I must go, for the child is ill.'

'Will you—will you come tomorrow?' he asked, unable to hide his anxiety and fear. He knew, at once, that in future he would reckon with her feelings, her thoughts, her desires—a new Mumbi. Again she considered his question for a little while.

'All right. Maybe I shall come,' she said and took her leave. She walked away with determined steps, sad but almost sure. He watched her until she disappeared at the door. Then he sank back to bed. He thought about the wedding gift, a stool carved from Muiri wood. 'I'll change the woman's figure. I shall curve a woman big—big with child.'

biographical information on african writers

ABRAHAMS, PETER. Born: Transvaal, South Africa, 1919. Mother: coloured; father: Ethiopian. Childhood: slum of Vrededorp in Johannesburg. Education: St. Peter's, Johannesburg. Publications: many novels. Now: lives in the West Indies, edits *West Indian Economist*.

ABRUQUAH, JOSEPH WILFRED. Born: Ghana. Education: Wesley College, Kumasi, Ghana; B.A. (Hons.) Degree and Dip.Ed. at King's College and Westminster College, London. Now: in the International Writing Program at University of Iowa. Publications: *The Catechist*, 1965 and *The Torrent*, 1968. Son of a catechist.

ACHEBE, CHINUA. Born: 1930, Eastern Nigeria. Father: catechist and teacher with the Church Missionary Society. Education: Government College in Umuahia; B.A. at University College, Ibadan. Occupations: 1954, broadcasting; 1961, Director of External Broadcasting in Nigeria. Four novels. Wife: Christie Okoli. Taught at Northwestern University African Studies Program. Spent much of the war in Biafra and on speaking tours in behalf of Biafra.

ALUKO, T. M. Born: 1918, Western Nigeria. Education: Ilesha and Government College, Ibadan; studied civil engineering and town planning in Lagos and London. In 1960 was appointed Director of Public Works for the Western Region of Nigeria. Now: with the staff of the University of Lagos. Three novels.

ARMAH, AYI KWEI. Born: Takoradi, Ghana, 1939. Has lived on coast, in interior forest region and in savannah north of Ghana. Education: Achimota school, Groton School in Massachusetts, Harvard (B.A. *cum laude* in Social Studies). M.A. in literature. translator in Algiers; television scriptwriter in Ghana; translator-editor on staff of *Jeune Afrique* in Paris; now teaching at University of Massachusetts.

DUODU, CAMERON. Born: 1937, Asiakwa, Ghana. 1960–1965: editor of *Drum* Magazine in Ghana. Had to flee the Nkrumah regime in 1965, went to London until *coup d'etat* in spring, 1966.

EKWENSI, CYPRIAN. Born in Northern Nigeria but belongs to the Ibo tribe. Education: Yaba Technical College, Lagos, in pharmacy. Former head of Features Dept., Nigerian Broadcasting Company. Until the Civil War, Director of Information Services for Nigeria. Many novels and short stories. During the Biafran war he was head of information. Since the surrender he has been trading inexpensive import items to make ends meet.

HONWANA, LUIS BERNARDO. Born: Lourenco Marques, Mozambique, 1942. The second of eight children, he attended the local primary school in Moamba, returned to Lourenco Marques for his High School education. A collection of his stories was published in Lourenco Marques in 1964.

KACHINGWE, AUBREY. Born: 1926. Malawian. Education: Malawi and Tanganyika. His uncle was an editor of a weekly newspaper in Blantyre. In 1950: cub reporter for the *East African Standard* group of newspapers in Nairobi. 1955: studied journalism in London and worked on foreign desk of *Daily Herald*. 1963: London B.B.C. in the African Service and News Department. Now head of News with the Malawi Broadcasting Corporation.

KAYIRA, LEGSON. Born: village, Malawi. Walked 2500 miles seeking education in U.S.A. Graduated from University of Washington. Now doing postgraduate work at Cambridge, England. Publications: three books.

LAYE, CAMARA. Born: 1924 in French Guinea. He grew up in a society where magic was an everyday event. Both his parents were believed to possess supernatural powers. Education: technical college at Conakry; engineering in France. Work: in a Simca factory in the suburbs of Paris while studying. Publications: several books.

MAIMANE, ARTHUR. Born: 1932, South Africa. Trained as a journalist there. Became Reuter's correspondent in East Africa. Worked for a time in Ghana. Went to England. Now works as a current affairs commentator for the B.B.C. Has had several plays broadcast and published many short stories.

MATTHEWS, JAMES. Born: 1929, Cape Town, South Africa. Eldest son of a poor and large family. First job: newspaper seller. After leaving high school, a messenger, journalist, and at present a telephonist. His collection of short stories, *Azilwewla*, has been published in Sweden.

MPHAHLELE, EZEKIEL. Born: 1919, in slums of Pretoria. Started school at 13 years of age. His childhood was spent carrying washing which his mother did for the white residents so that her three children might eat and gain an education. He finished high school, taught English and Afrikaans. Dismissed from school for his opposition to Bantu Education. Received external degrees of B.A. and M.A. from University of South Africa. Not allowed to teach. Stories, *Man Must Live*, were published in 1947; autobiography, *Down Second Avenue* was published in 1959; his master's thesis, *The African Image* in 1962. Taught in Nigeria, worked in Paris, Geneva, Denver and East Africa.

NGUGI, JAMES. Born: Highlands of Kenya. Education: University College, Makerere. Occupation: Journalist in Nairobi. University of Leeds. Several novels and plays. Teaches at University of Makerere.

NKOSI, LEWIS. Born: Johannesburg, South Africa. Occupation: journalist and broadcaster. Worked on *Drum* and other magazines. Eventually left South Africa for political reasons. Many published articles.

OYONO, FERDINAND. Born: 1929, Cameroons. Educated there and in France. Appeared on stage in the title role of Louis Sapin's *Papa Bon Dieu* at the Theatre d'Aujourd'hui in Paris. Now in the Diplomatic Service, first in Paris, then Rome, then at the United Nations, now in Brussels. Two novels translated into English.

RABEARIVELO, JEAN-JOSEPH. Born: 1901, at Antananarivo, Madagascar, of poor parents. With very little formal schooling he taught himself French and Spanish and wrote poetry in both languages as well as in his native Malagasy. He worked as a publisher's clerk and published several volumes of poetry. In spite of his devotion to French culture, he was never able to visit France. He committed suicide in 1937. From 1930–31 he was co-editor of an interesting but short-lived literary review, *Capri corne*.

SOYINKA, WOLFE. Born: 1935 in Abeokuta, Nigeria. Studied at University College, Ibadan. Read for English honors degree at Leeds University. Returned to Nigeria in 1960 to staff of the University of Ife. Many plays, poems, and one novel. Early in the Biafran war he was imprisoned by the Lagos regime as a security risk (he tried to visit Biafra), was released in October 1969 under a general amnesty. Now he is reorganizing the drama department at the University of Ibadan and filming his play, *Kongi's Harvest*. In the summer of 1970 he produced a play, *Madmen and Specialists*, written in prison, at Connecticut's O'Neill Theater, following previews in the black areas of Hartford, New Haven and Waterford.